The Teenage Foster Carer's Handbook

Caring for young people in foster and residential care and helping them to become adults

Ann Wheal
with
Meral Mehmet

Russell House Publishing

First published in 1994 by Longman as *Answers for Carers*
Second edition 1999 by Pavilion as *Answers for Carers*
Third edition 2003 by Russell House Publishing as *Young People in Foster and Residential Care*
This fourth edition by:
Russell House Publishing Ltd.
58 Broad Street
Lyme Regis
Dorset DT7 3QF
Tel: 01297 443948
Fax: 01297 442722
e-mail: help@russellhouse.co.uk
www.russellhouse.co.uk

Please see page x for the special and restricted photocopying permission granted for this work
and page x for the discount purchase of The Teenager's Foster Carer's Handbook and the
loose-leaf version of it.

British Library Cataloguing-in-publication Data:
A catalogue record for this book is available from the British Library.

ISBN: 978-1-905541-81-2
Design and layout by Jeremy Spencer
Printed by IQ Laserpress, Aldershot

About Russell House Publishing
Russell House Publishing aims to publish innovative and valuable materials to help
managers, practitioners, trainers, educators and students.

Our full catalogue covers: families, children and young people; engagement and inclusion;
drink, drugs and mental health; textbooks in youth work and social work; workforce
development.

Full details can be found at **www.russellhouse.co.uk** and we are pleased to send out
information to you by post. Our contact details are on this page.

We are always keen to receive feedback on publications and new ideas for future projects.

Contents

About this book

Who is the book for?

This handbook has been produced for foster carers who are working with young people, and will also be helpful to residential carers and anyone working with young people who have left, or who will shortly be leaving, care.

How the book works

This book has been developed:
- For young people and carers to read together.
- To provide carers with answers to questions they may have about bringing up a young person aged 11-18.
- To help carers answer the many questions a young person aged 11-18 may ask about their time being looked after and when they leave care.
- To be used as a 'talking tool' when carers are working in partnership with young people, either in groups or one-to-one. In this way young people will learn to take responsibility for their own future.

The book may be used as a way to start talking with young people about issues that extend beyond the home. Whilst this book covers some aspects of being a carer and carers' responsibilities, the primary focus is the direct work with young people. The authors suggest *The Foster Carer's Handbook* would be a good resource for the former. See page xii.

Throughout the book there are examples of questions that a young person might ask, along with some suggested answers.

Checklists and extra information that will only be of interest to particular young people at particular times have also been included. These have been written as though they are for the young person and may be photocopied on the terms laid out on pages ii and x.

No mention has been made of benefits entitlement as these vary with individual circumstances.

This handbook has been written so that it may also be useful for carers being assessed and for those undertaking childcare placements and qualifications as part of their qualifying or post qualifying courses.

The underlying ethos of the Handbook is in line with The Children Act (1989), the Children (Scotland) Act (1995) and the Children's Order (Northern Ireland) (1995) as well as the additional relevant Acts that have been passed since that time. It is designed to:
- Encourage carers to work in partnership with the young people in their care.
- Encourage young people to return to their parents' home as soon as possible, if appropriate.
- Encourage those looking after the young people to work with them in all sorts of ways, so that they will be able to take their place in society in the future.

See page 2 for further commentary on standards in the various parts of the UK.

This book will seek to ensure that there is no discrimination on the grounds of age, gender, disability (including use of sign language), race, ethnic origin, nationality, sexual orientation, social class, religion or language.

Copying permission

Purchasers of *The Teenager's Foster Carer's Handbook* are allowed to undertake incidental photocopying when working at various times with any individual young person on just two or three pages to meet specific needs that arise.

If you want to make multiple copies of a few pages, please check whether that is permitted under your licence with the Copyright Licencing Agency, if you have one. If you are uncertain about this, you must seek permission from the publisher at help@ russellhouse.co.uk or on 01297 443948.

No material may be resold or posted on the internet.

Discount purchase

Loose leaf version

We have found that many organisations want to provide their carers with the information contained in this book but also wish to add local details, procedures and forms. To help with this, we can supply *The Teenager's Foster Carer's Handbook* as loose-leaf sets which you can incorporate with your own materials in your own folders to form a comprehensive resource pack for local use.

Discounts

We can offer substantial discounts on bulk purchases of either the book itself or loose-leaf sets.

Please contact us for an up to date quote or to discuss your particular needs: **we're here to help**.

Tel: 01297 443948
Fax: 01297 442722
e-mail: help@russellhouse.co.uk
Russell House Publishing
58 Broad Street
Lyme Regis DT7 3QF

What readers have said about previous editions of this book

...a very good handbook for new foster carers, full of useful information and easy to understand (the best yet!).

foster carer

I was particularly impressed that there is a distinct lack of jargon. It certainly made the introduction of our latest foster child very easy.

foster carer

Use of the handbook was very good as a back up to what I had already explained to the client. I could then show the client and they could read it easily to confirm my decision. Open discussions amongst the children are great. They can air their grievances etc. which can help a sometimes explosive situation. Involving the clients builds up interest, self-esteem etc. – very good.

care assistant

...extremely useful for in-house training for staff, residents, foster carers and clients; supervision with staff and residents; staff meetings and residents' meetings; a quick reference for service users, families and friends. Available for residents, families, friends and community.

residential carer

I found this handbook excellent, the most informative information I've ever received, both for myself and the young people I care for.

foster carer

...very useful for NVQ (SNVQ) and social care related courses.

residential manager

A book like this could ensure that all staff have some training, whatever the level they are employed at.

student

About the authors

Ann Wheal was a teacher in inner-city schools and colleges before working at the University of Southampton in the Social Work division. Her areas of research were children in care and children leaving care. Ann has been a governor at a special needs nursery and a volunteer in a secure unit. She has published widely in the area of children and families.

Meral Mehmet is a freelance social work consultant with 30 years' experience in social care of which 20 years has been in fostering. She has worked with a variety of fostering providers and in a range of fostering and child care related roles, including for social care in Turkey and UNICEF. Meral has for the past 12 years been a freelance consultant and trainer and for the past five years a tutor at Middlesex University.

By the same authors

The FOSTER CARER'S Handbook

For carers of children 11 years and under

Acclaimed across three previous editions, this handbook can help anyone looking after children aged approximately 11 years and under, including those with special needs, to provide care that equals or surpasses what is required.

Primarily for foster carers, but also useful in residential care, it is packed with detailed guidance about looking after children, being looked after, being a foster carer and living in a fostering household. It explains the law, procedures and roles of everyone involved; and gives detailed advice on how to manage the numerous large and small things needing attention in any child's life – education, health, money, relationships and much more. It aims to:

- Encourage carers to work in partnership with the children and their families
- Enable children to return to their families when appropriate _ Enable carers to meet the full range of a child's needs _ Explain the fostering roles and responsibilities.

Although there are differences in detail, the governments of England, Scotland, Wales and Northern Ireland all make similar requirements of carers. This book aims to help all carers achieve the expectations placed on them and maintain standards. It underlines and encourages the use of relevant government standards, and gives examples of good practice.

A comprehensive guide that can be called on when just about anything arises, it has been developed:

- For carers to read themselves along with the children they are caring for as well as their own children.
- To help carers make appropriate decisions, and answer the many questions children may ask about their time 'being looked after'.
- For use as a 'talking tool': it includes photocopiable supporting activities to help children understand the present, face the future with confidence and, in time, make their own decisions about their life.
- For use in supervision and training.

A4 paperback. 232 pages. 978-1-905541-77-5. Published Jan 2012. £29.95.

Acknowledgements

In 1992 the Department of Social Work Studies at the University of Southampton took part in a research project which became known as the Dolphin Project. During the project, Ann Wheal and Daphne Walder met young people who were being looked after in Birmingham, Berkshire and Hampshire. They told us what they knew about the Children Act and also about their time in children's homes and in foster care. Ann Buchanan also met their carers.

A report called *Answering Back: A Young Person's View of the Children Act* was published. The first edition of this book was one off the many outcomes of this report.

There is a similar book for carers of children under 11 years entitled *The Foster Carer's Handbook* by Ann Wheal and Meral Mehmet published by Russell House Publishing (opposite).

Many people helped in so many ways with the previous editions by assisting with funding; being members of our working party; acting as critical readers; advisers and evaluators and the young people themselves who made suggestions and criticisms very willingly. We are extremely grateful to each and every one of them for their valued contribution.

We would particularly like to thank Ann Buchanan who was deeply involved in the first edition of this book and without whom Ann would probably not have started writing in the first place. We would also like to thank the following who helped with this book:

Jan Bambridge, Family Placement Team, West Sussex City Council; Allena Doley, Senior Dental Officer, Solent Healthcare Service; Angela Elliott, Senior Projects Manager (Children's Services), London Borough of Ealing; Ena Fry, MBE, Independent Consultant; Diane Heath, Regional Consultant (London and South East) The Fostering Network; Nick Henney, Independent Reviewing Officer, London Borough of Islington; Alyza Johnson, Deputy Head, Fordwater School, Chichester; Eve Lemm, Senior Avisory Teacher, Inclusion Support Team, West Sussex County Council; Claire Lewis, Acting Team Manager, Child Disability Team, West Sussex County Council.

We would also like to especially thank our husbands Peter and Kemal for their help, patience and guidance.

Ann Wheal and Meral Mehmet
2012

Section 1
Background

Inch by inch: helping young people to succeed

This handbook has been produced primarily for foster carers but also has useful information for those working in residential care. It is aimed at those who are looking after young people over the age of 11 years.

The handbook aims to ensure that we always keep the interests of young people as our focus which includes listening to them whenever necessary and developing our skills to be able do so. Young people should be placed within their family or with close friends or relatives where possible: fostering or residential care should be considered only when it is really necessary.

How to use this handbook

It is not possible to learn to become a good carer by reading a book. This book should be used as **a guide, referred to as necessary or dipped into when a particular topic arises**.

It can also be used as a supervision tool by the foster carer and their supervising social worker for training purposes and as a reminder of fostering standards.

Foster carers should find it useful to use with their own children who should find the information and ideas offered very helpful. It is important that your own children understand the responsibilities of fostering, such as issues of confidentiality. At the same time, it is essential that they are listened to and included in decisions made that will affect them as well as the young people placed with you.

Some adults think that if young people are given too much information it may be misused, but our experience points to the reverse. The more information young people have the better able they will be to successfully plan their future lives as adults.

Some of the terms in the book may vary from region to region, however the overriding principles are the same.

Everyone needs to be valued, to feel special, and to feel important. By treating all young people as individuals, working with, and caring for them, a carer can make a huge impact on a young person's life. Quite often, it is a small thing that you do or don't do that has the greatest impact on them. For example, at one time there was much publicity about the practice of using black plastic sacks to transport a young person's property and treasured possessions from one house to the next. This practice, which shows a total lack of respect for them and young person's belongings, has, hopefully now stopped. Frank Dobson, a Minister of Health in the 1990s, once suggested that when talking about practice for looked after children, we should ask ourselves, 'is it good enough for my child?'

All practice should be based on ensuring that 'it is good enough for my child'. We hope this book will help.

All this doesn't happen overnight. Young people need to be taught skills to help them make decisions and when these decisions turn out to be wrong, how to pick up the pieces and start again, no matter how painful it is.

He, who has never made a mistake, has never made anything.

This old saying is true of us all, and the young people in your care need your time and patience as well as all the information you can give them to help them make informed choices and sensible decisions about their lives.

**A good carer is someone who sits down and listens to you
and discusses things with you.**
young person's view

Standards in foster care

The way England, Wales, Scotland and Northern Ireland have been devolved over the past years has resulted in variations in the way each country takes responsibility for social care. This has led to some marked differences, and one such is in the requirement to work with nationally proscribed standards. Please refer specifically to the website for each country's government department for more details. BAAF and the Fostering Network also work across the four countries, and are able to give more details.

Although there are differences in detail, the governments of England, Scotland, Wales and Northern Ireland all require that carers understand:
- The principles and values essential for fostering children and young people.
- Their role as a foster carer.
- Health and safety and health care.
- How to communicate effectively with children.
- The development of children and young people.
- How to keep children and young people safe from harm.
- The importance of self-development.

The aim of this book is to:
- Help all carers achieve the expectations placed on them and maintain good standards.
- Underline and encourage the use of relevant government standards.
- Give examples of good practice.

Section 2

Who Cares?

All fostering agencies, as a matter of good practice, should give foster carers clear details of the role, task and responsibilities they will have when caring for children. This section brings together the spirit of the current legislation with good practice in UK. It also lists a range of professionals and their role.

The Fostering Network recommend that we consider matters in terms of competencies for foster carers under the following headings:
- Caring for children.
- Providing a safe and caring environment.
- Working as part of a team.
- Being responsible for your own development.

The following carer's role and task description is based on the one produced by the Fostering Network. We have focussed on some of the specific areas necessary for young people.

Carers' responsibilities

A carer should be able to:
- Provide each young person with nutrition, food, clothing, a bed and a small personal area, or separate room if possible.
- Include each young person in the activities of the home.
- Establish clear expectations and limits.
- Discipline fairly.
- Deal with negative behaviour in a positive way.
- Reward good behaviour.
- Promote and encourage a relationship with the birth family.
- Encourage a young person's cultural and religious heritage and behave in a way which does not discriminate.
- Arrange for routine and emergency medical and dental care.
- Assume responsibility for the young person's daily school activities.
- Ensure that the young person's educational needs are met.
- Promote a young person's self-esteem and positive self-image.
- Respect the young person and their birth family.
- Work with all concerned, including the young person, to make a permanent plan for them.
- Help prepare the young person to return to their birth family, or be placed with relatives, friends, or adoptive parents, or to live independently.
- Help the young person to speak up, to be heard and to be listened to.
- To listen, to understand and to relate to each young person.

There may be other things you think should be added to this list.

Young people want their carers to:
- Share information with them about their rights under the law and make sure that they fully understand any legal order affecting them.
- Acknowledge difference whether due to disability, racial origin, language, religion or culture; respect and support young people and challenge discrimination.
- Provide opportunities for young people to make choices and to learn about making decisions and involve them in planning.
- Help young people in their relationships with their parents.
- Help young people to participate in their reviews.
- Prepare young people for independence.
- Share information about pocket money and allowances.
- Support young people in making a complaint.
- Help young people develop other relationships, other partnerships and make decisions to allow them to stay overnight with friends.
- Advocate for young people in obtaining equal access in education.
- Recognise and support young people when they are in distress.

Foster care agreement

The foster care agreement can be seen as a work contract. It should contain a range of information including the terms and conditions that carers will be working under and what the fostering service should be providing for carers to enable them to carry out their role in the care of young people. All carers should have their own, signed, copy which should be up-to-date and easy to read.

Support groups

Foster carers should know about, and use where necessary, the different support groups available. They should also identify people in their network who they would be able to trust to take care of the young person for short periods of time. The fostering service should ensure that these people are supported and positively encouraged.

Allegations against carers

Unfortunately some carers will have allegations made against them. Having an allegation made against a carer is one of the most stressful experiences possible. It is essential therefore that the carer operates clear house rules and a safer caring policy in the home – see page 26.

There are clearly set out procedures regarding how allegations are investigated and it is quite likely that you will only know of an allegation once the process of the investigation has started. It will indicate why and how an investigation will be carried out. You should also receive in writing, specific details regarding what is going to happen to you and time frames by which the investigation should be conducted.

The carer should be informed of the allegation as soon as possible and their views obtained. The carer also has the right to be supported by an independent person.

Why a young person might make an allegation against a carer:
- Something that has happened recently reminds the young person of an event that took place before they came to live with the carer.
- It is a way for the young person to try to regain control over their life.
- The young person sees it as a way of getting back home by making a false accusation.
- The young person can misinterpret an innocent action, such as the carer putting an arm around them to offer comfort.

However, most significantly, it may be that the young person is being treated badly or being abused. Unfortunately this may happen in foster care.

? *What can carers do to help prevent accusations being made against them?*

Carers should always follow the safer carer guidelines which suggests they should:
- Be open with the young person and explain what you are doing and why.
- Keep a diary listing the main happenings for the day – it will be a very useful record in its own right regardless of the possibility of an accusation being made against you – and it could prove invaluable if you are wrongly accused.
- Help young people learn to say **NO** if they don't want to be touched.
- Give those young people who may need it, extra help in working out how to seek comfort from an adult without clinging to them or being fearful.
- Avoid tickling and wrestling games if it is likely that the young person will misinterpret such a game until the young person is able to understand and enjoy this interaction in a healthy way.
- Let young people who are old enough bathe and wash by themselves.
- Ensure that all young people in the house have dressing gowns and slippers and should wear them when walking around the house in their night-clothes.
- Not share their bed with a young person even if the young person is ill.
- Provide young people with a time of warmth and affection outside the bedroom, telling stories, reading, talking or having a hot drink together.
- Not let young people share beds with other children or young people. If young people share bedrooms, clear rules should apply.
- Prevent young people from developing sexual feelings for their carers or members of the carer's family by openly discussing topics such as sex, feelings, emotions and relationships as they occur.

You may be the last person to know that an allegation has been made against you! In fact you may only find out when the police knock on your door! Start keeping records now – don't get caught out.

? *What should I do if I am accused of abuse?*

If an allegation is made, carers should call the member of their family or support network – whoever is most likely to be able to help – and contact their professional association and their local authority. Foster Care Associations or support groups should also be able to help. Carers will need advice from a solicitor with experience of dealing with abuse cases.

Complaints against carers

Although some complaints against carers may ultimately turn out to be very serious, the majority will be about standards of care such as issues about pocket money, clothing, use of the Internet etc. Every effort should be made to resolve these types of issues in meetings between the carer, the young person and relevant social workers.

If the complaint is found to be false, then your supervising social worker will support you to ensure that the record of the outcome of the complaint is recorded accurately, and also to advise how such situations may be prevented in the future.

Men who foster

Men who foster can have an influential role in the lives of the young people they look after. Many young people will have previously experienced father figures as absent, or abusive, and they may have confused expectations of a male foster carer. All carers, male and female, need to think about the role of male foster carers, and the positive impact that they can have on fostered young people.

Most men who foster do so in partnership with a woman, but a minority do so as single male carers or in same sex relationships. Some men may be home-based and the main carer, while others may fulfil the more traditional role of family providers, employed full-time outside the home. Whatever the working arrangements are, men and women who foster are both responsible for the day-to-day care offered to young people, and for communication with other professionals.

Fathers' involvement in young people's lives can have a positive impact on their self-esteem, self-control, sociability, empathy and educational development. This involvement may take the form of substantial periods of time spent with young people, in caring, play, helping with schoolwork, and sharing leisure activities. Sadly, more than half of fathers in the UK appear to spend less than five minutes a day individually with their own children. Foster fathers' involvement has therefore been seen to have a positive impact on the mental health of young people, as well as contributing to greater placement stability. Men who foster offer a role model for young men and women. Foster fathers themselves identify some aspects of this 'positive male role model' as:
- A safe, caring, non-threatening male.
- Showing a range of feelings and emotions (not just anger).
- Challenging stereotypes of men and women.

It is great for the young person if the male carer:
- Spends individual time with fostered young people and acts as a good role model.
- Takes an active interest in young people's education, health, and leisure activities.
- Is involved in joint decision making with his partner (if there is one) about fostering issues.
- Is included in all placement planning meetings.
- Meets regularly with social workers and other professionals.

Practical guidelines for men who foster

- Understand the pattern of abuse a young person has previously suffered, and ask questions of the social worker – normal family routines can then be realistically adapted.
- Agree with the social worker how daily routines such as bedtimes and bath times should be approached based on the individual young person's needs to allow the foster father to give nurturing care if needed.
- Offer positive time with young people – outings, leisure pursuits, help with homework, reading. Again, be clear with other professionals that this is ordinary family life and take advice on whether there are any particular risks attached.
- Offer young people comfortable safe alternatives to manage sexualised behaviour. Don't avoid all intimacy – make it safe for youngsters. As a family, allow and create opportunities to discuss issues like sexuality, sexual abuse and emotions.
- Always keep a written record of significant incidents and signs that you have noticed. Be clear with the social worker what recording is required. Talk openly with your partner (if you have one) especially about your feelings and reactions to the fostered young person. If you are concerned about behaviour let professionals know at the time, not weeks afterwards.

Insurance for carers

All carers **must** ensure that they and their household (anyone over the age of 18 years) have insurance cover. All carers should be provided with adequate public liability and professional indemnity protection which should cover claims made by a young person as well as any other issues arising from the fostering task. Carers must take responsibility for getting information in writing of the insurance cover their agency may have taken out for them or other arrangements put in place by the fostering service provider and for finding out how their *own* insurance is affected if they foster.

The Foster Care Agreement should contain clear explanations regarding the agency's arrangements for meeting any legal liabilities that are a result of fostering. The arrangements must also include how the agency will meet claims by, or against foster carers, in respect of damage, loss or injury, or legal defence costs particularly to cover child abuse claims.

Training and guidance for carers and social workers

Training plays a very important part in a carer's development. It begins with training to become a foster carer, and continues throughout the person's career on a wide variety of topics. It may lead to qualifications if the carer wishes or if it is the policy of the agency to have qualified carers.

Vocational qualifications

NVQ stands for National Vocational Qualification, SVQ in Scotland. It is a 'competence-based' qualification: this means you learn practical, work-related tasks designed to help develop the skills and knowledge to do a job effectively.

NVQs are based on national standards for various occupations. The standards say what a competent person in a job could be expected to do. As you progress through the course, you compare your skills and knowledge with these standards as you learn, so you can see what you need to do to meet them. The approach to NVQ/SVQs varies. Some local authorities and Independent Fostering Agencies (IFAs) give all their carers the opportunity to work towards this award.

GNVQs (General National Vocational Qualifications) and AVCEs (Advanced Vocational Certificates of Education) are school or college courses which can be taken on their own or alongside A levels or GCSEs. GNVQ/AVCEs are not meant to train a person for a specific job but to teach knowledge and skills that can be applied to broad career such as social care.

? What other qualifications are there?

Some carers having achieved their NVQ move on to higher education and study for a variety of qualifications including academic degrees.

It is good practice to ensure that foster care training will also include joint training with supervising social workers. Equally training which includes young people and the foster carer's own children should be developed.

Employer training

Employers offer a wide variety of courses. Employees, including foster carers, may be required to attend some of them such as 'safe handling' whilst others may be chosen to fit in with the carer's career aspirations and development. Many of the courses award points which can be put towards a specific qualification such as NVQ, GNVQ or a degree.

Social work degree

BA or BSc in social work. The professional qualification for social workers is an honours degree that must include a minimum of 200 days spent in practice settings.

Students learn about child and adult development, psychology, and why people get into the situations they do. Law, criminal justice, social policy, anti-discrimination, social work and interviewing skills are other components of the degree. Students usually specialise in their final year – perhaps with young people, or adults with special needs. Joint honours courses allow students to study areas such as community development, health care and youth studies.

Post-qualifying training

Following a variety of government initiatives aimed at setting standards and improving practice, a UK Child Care Award for qualified social workers has been developed.

The award provides a qualification for professional child care social workers from many diverse settings. The requirements for the award focus on the assessment of the developmental needs of young people and the capacity of parents and care-givers to respond to these needs. They take into account the impact the wider family and environmental factors have on the development of the child or young person and on parenting capacity.

The Child Care Award provides evidence that successful candidates have the skills and knowledge to be able to:

- Assess the developmental needs of young people and the capacity of parents or carers to meet those needs.
- Use research findings to underpin practice.
- Use professional judgement in reaching decisions about young people in need.
- Work within an inter-agency framework.
- Co-ordinate the delivery of planned services and evaluate their effectiveness.
- Work effectively within legal and policy frameworks.
- Contribute to corporate and strategic planning.
- Work with diverse communities and groups, and be able to communicate complicated circumstances and identify gaps in services.

Registration of social workers

Anyone who wishes to practise as a social worker in England, Wales, Scotland or Northern Ireland must register with the registration council for their particular country which usually lasts for three years. They must also undertake at least 15 days training in each three years of their registration which may take the form of research, work shadowing, developing good practice policies in a relevant field or studying for a certified higher education qualification.

At present foster carers, unlike other care workers, are not required to register with their relevant social care council but there are many who think that this should, and will, change in the future.

Who's who in helping young people

Below is a list of some of those involved with young people. They may be known by other names in different regions.

Key worker
In residential settings the key workers are responsible for the young people. They build a relationship with the young person, assess their needs, and help to meet those needs. They are involved with admissions; planning; liaising with other agencies and with parents and for the overall well-being of the young person.

Key worker's line manager, supervisor, team manager or head of home
This is the person who is responsible for the key worker. Key workers will go to their line manager for advice and guidance. This person may be the manager of the home. If a young person has any difficulties with their key worker, the child should discuss this with another worker or the line manager.

Children's social worker (CSW)
All young people who are being looked after will have a social worker. Generally speaking, their job is to keep in touch with the young person, and others involved with the young person and to make sure the young person's care plan is carried out. They attend planning meetings and reviews, and handle court matters.

Team managers/area managers/directors

Most children's departments are organised like pyramids, with team managers, area managers and finally the director. Each level is responsible for the level below. It is a good idea to find out how your local services are organised as you might need the help of someone very senior.

Supervising social worker (SSW)

Most foster carers will have their own social worker who is based in the fostering team. This person advises and supports the foster carer and the foster carer's household on general fostering issues but also with ensuring the child's plan and their overall needs are met.

Independent reviewing officer (IRO)

It is the role of the IRO to ensure that the best plans are made for, and where the child is old enough to contribute, *with* the child. They will chair and produce minutes of all the child's reviews and will ensure the agreements reached at the end of each review are carried out. They have a very crucial role in the welfare of children, for instance, they can prevent a child from being unnecessarily moved from a stable placement if they do not think this to be in the young person's interests. They can also take matters further if they feel that a young person is being unnecessarily denied access to services or resources.

Other helpers who may be involved:

Children's rights officer (CRO)

Children's rights are laid down by the UN Convention on the Rights of the Child. Young people in residential and foster care should be able to telephone the CRO and discuss in confidence anything that is bothering them in the certain knowledge that their complaints will be listened to and dealt with. Young people should also be able to contact Childline or similar organisations.

It is important that young people know what their rights are and how they can exercise those rights. This includes their right to challenge decisions and to question the way in which services are provided for them.

Independent visitor

An independent visitor is someone who may be appointed if it is thought a young person needs a specific person who can visit, befriend, take them out or act in some ways as a mentor, perhaps because their own parents are not around or do not visit.

Advocate

An advocate is a person who speaks up for a young person. They may find out information that a young person needs or they may try to get things changed on behalf of a young person. They may also attend reviews or planning meetings if they are invited by the young person. Much of what they do will be similar to an independent person but they are not appointed by the local authority but chosen by the young person. Some organisations such as The Voice offer an advocacy service for young people.

Mentor

A mentor is a person (often a volunteer) who is available to give advice and encouragement during particular periods in a young person's life, such as leaving care and trying to find a job. Mentoring seeks to realise and fulfil the potential of a young person, to develop their skills and help promote new opportunities for them.

Personal adviser

All young people should have access to a personal adviser who is often part of the careers service. They should ensure that the needs of each young person are met and that they are motivated to engage in education, training or work opportunities to achieve their full potential.

Young people leaving care may also have a personal adviser who is part of the leaving care team.

Children's Commissioner

The Commissioner is a champion for all children and young people but especially for those most at risk of exclusion and deprivation. They usually have countrywide responsibilities, and governments have a say in their appointment.

The four main areas of work are:
1. Promoting and safeguarding children's rights.
2. Communicating with young people.
3. Investigations and complaints.
4. Promoting good practice.

Complaints officer

Every local authority must have a complaints officer who is responsible for investigating complaints. There is a clearly set out process for investigating these matters and one of the responsibilities of a complaints officer is to ensure that the young person who has made a complaint is kept informed of progress and of the eventual outcome of any investigation.

Children's Guardian (England and Wales) and Curator Ad Litem or Safeguarder (Scotland)

These are people who are appointed to promote the rights and welfare of children who are the subject of care proceedings. They will actively seek the views of young people. They write reports which are used as part of the process of deciding what is in the young person's best interest.

Education social workers

Their job is to be a link between the school and the residential or foster home. They talk to the school about problems a young person may be experiencing, for example bullying. They are also involved if a young person is truanting.

Educational psychologist

If a young person is having difficulties in learning or concentrating at school, the head teacher may ask for an educational psychologist to see them. An educational psychologist is someone who has special knowledge about how young people learn and what may be causing them to have difficulties.

Child and family workers and child therapists

Child and family workers and child therapists help young people who may have an emotional or behavioural problem, for instance because of some earlier unhappy experience at home. A child psychiatrist will be part of the team which includes psychologists and specialist social workers.

And of course … foster carers

Foster carers provide many different types of care either short term or long term. Specialist foster carers have specific skills, for instance to look after teenagers, young people with disabilities or those with behavioural problems. Foster carers also have responsibilities to themselves, so …

> Look after yourself and always plan something for you.
>
> Plan time with your partner.
>
> Plan something you enjoy doing with your children.
>
> Use the support networks and resources offered to you.

Section 3
Being Looked After

Settling in

When a young person first enters care they will probably have been under considerable stress and it is very important that this early stage is well planned and carefully handled.

Each young person is different and will need to be treated differently. They may want, for example:
- To be on their own.
- To talk to you alone.
- To talk to another young person.
- To very quickly become one of the 'family' and pretend everything is fine.

Quite often they may be rude or aggressive or even totally silent and not eat. Whatever their reaction in the first few days let them be alone – yet not alone – be alert, watch and observe and be there when needed. Gradually try to persuade them to take part in the life of their new home. Give them a welcoming, warm environment. Explain what is going on, why they are there, and if you know, how long for.

Tell them how the system works, who is responsible for them and who they can go to if they need help.

Let them tell you about their previous experience, where they lived and what the rules were. This will give you an opportunity to discuss your own rules and the ones they are used to.

? What's happening to me?
The young person in your care may be confused about who's who, and what is happening to them. (There is a list of who's who in Section 2 and Section 14 covers the legal aspects).

If young people are confused:
- Explain what a social worker does.
- What their court order means if they have one.
- What the many new terms they will hear mean.
- Why they cannot be with their parents and when they might see them or their siblings.

It will help to make them feel more secure and to settle more easily. Your job in the first few days is to help them pick up the pieces of their lives.

Encourage them to:
- Go back to school or college as soon as possible.
- Make contact with their family (if that's possible) and friends.
- Talk through with you what has happened.
- Talk about what interests them.

Don't be put off if you are rejected at first. Try again. Try a different approach. Gradually they'll come round and want to talk. It may be particularly difficult for young people with disabilities or those from different cultures and backgrounds.

Meetings

Meetings, meetings, meetings. There are so many different meetings which often seem to be a waste of time. However, meetings are useful for:

- Obtaining information.
- Sharing views.
- Solving problems.
- Reaching decisions.
- Making plans.
- Checking progress.
- Gaining consensus.

To be effective, meetings need to achieve their aim in a reasonable way in a reasonable time, leaving a trail of clear crisp decisions. However, to really be effective, young people need to fully participate or at least appreciate how important the various meetings are to them. The following are some of the ones that are particularly important but, before that, it is important for carers to know about delegated authority.

Delegated authority (DA)

A foster carer can be given delegated authority (DA) for the child they are caring for either by the child's parents or, if a child is on either an interim or a full care order, the local authority. Delegated authority is the consent to take decisions for a child on a number of matters. These include issues regarding their health, including routine checks and appointments; their education, including school trips and school activities and such things as sports, holidays, overnight stays, hair cuts etc. These matters will be discussed at the placement planning meeting which should be held either in advance of the placement or within five days of the placement. It is necessary to discuss these matter early on to ensure that the child can participate in 'normal' family activities and limits their feelings of being different from other children.

The placement plan

Placement planning meetings

These are meetings where the young person's placement plan is completed. The placement plan is part of the child's care plan and should usually be completed before a placement begins or within five days of it starting. The placement plan goes through day-to-day and practical arrangements for the young person, and the young person's parents (or anyone else with parental responsibilities for the young person) need to be present because agreements and consents need to be finalised. Such agreements and consents spell out what a foster carer may or may not allow the young person to do. This includes matters such as joining in certain activities, which may involve risk, getting the young person's hair cut or enabling the young person to be immunised.

Sometimes these consents and agreements will be referred to as delegated authority (DA). It is important to understand that only those with parental responsibility (PR) can give such consents and agreements. They will usually be a young person's parents who have PR although PR can be given through the courts to others caring for a young person; or if the young person is on an interim care order or a full care order, PR is shared with the local authority.

The placement plan, as with other documents relating to a young person, needs to be regularly reviewed to ensure the young person is not missing out on activities or being denied services unnecessarily. Much of what is contained in the placement plan is directed at enabling young people who are accommodated to live as normal a life as possible. Young people should contribute to these meetings and there will be times when a young person will be able to override objections, for instance from their parents regarding an activity, if they are considered to be old enough and mature enough to make such decisions themselves.

Those attending a placement planning meeting would include:
- the young person
- the young person's social worker
- the foster carer
- the supervising social worker
- the young person's parents or carers

The areas covered in the placement planning meeting are similar to those set out for meetings below and include arrangements for the young person's:
- health
- education
- leisure
- contact
- other day to day matters such as the use of the internet or a mobile phone, pocket money, bedtime routines etc.

The care plan

Every young person must have an up-to-date plan so that they know where they stand and what it is hoped will happen to them in the future. They should take part in making this plan which will then have their commitment. In some cases an interpreter may be needed, but in all cases it is important the young person understands and can contribute as fully as they wish. Your local authority will give you guidance on this. If the young person does not have a plan, you should press for one to be prepared as soon as possible.

2 *What will be in the care plan?*
- What the young person's needs are, including health, diet, religion, language, education, friends.
- If a young person is disabled, what extra help they need.
- Where the young person will be living.
- If it is possible to predict how long they are likely to be in care.
- What will happen in the future, and when it will happen?
- When and if the young person will see their parents, and how the parents will be involved.

- What will happen if things don't work out as planned.
- Arrangements for education, health care and other matters important to the young person.
- Who is responsible for carrying out the various aspects of the care plan and by when.

? *Who goes to a planning meeting?*

Whenever possible:
- the young person
- parents
- the social worker
- anyone else who cares about the young person such as grandparents, aunts, uncles, friends
- anyone who works with the young person, such as the manager of a children's home
- foster carer/key worker
- the supervising social worker
- other people may be invited such as legal advisors, teachers, doctors, educational social workers

? *Can a young person speak at the meeting?*

Yes. Encourage the young person to say what they think and to be part of any decisions made. The young person should be prepared before the meeting so they can take an active part in discussions. Young people may ask for some members of the group to leave the room for a time if they feel uncomfortable speaking in front of them.

? *What happens next?*

The agreed plan and any decisions made in the meeting will be written down and everybody who was invited should be given a copy, including the young person. Further planning meetings may be called later to see how things are progressing. As it is not always easy to put the plan into action quickly, carers will need to tell the young person how things are progressing as well as to encourage the young person to talk about any worries. See page 122.

Young people's reviews

Young people should be encouraged to attend their reviews whenever possible and if they can't attend, to send their comments. Reviews are where important decisions about a young person's plans take place. The young person's social worker is responsible for organising their review and should make sure that the time and place is suitable for everyone especially the young person – it is after all their review. A young person can ask for a review to take place. The young person's social worker should talk with them to see if there is anyone they do not want to attend the meeting and how this might be managed.

? *What are children's reviews?*

Reviews are regular meetings which children's services must hold for all young people who are looked after by them.

A review is held:
- To ensure a young person is being cared for properly.
- To make sure that the plans made for the young person are being carried out.
- To decide whether the plans should be changed in any way.

? How often do they happen?

They are held within four weeks of when a young person is first looked after but may be held earlier, and then within three months, and then within six months. If a lot is happening or there is a problem, then reviews may be held more often.

? Must the young person go to them?

It's a very good idea for the young person to attend as they can have their say about what's going on. Encourage the young person to speak up for themselves and complain or make suggestions.

The young person can take a friend or someone else they trust and can also get that person to speak on their behalf if they find talking in front of everyone difficult. If it really isn't possible for the young person to attend their review they can write down what they want to say and ask someone else to read it for them.

? Who will be there?

All the people who are concerned about the young person should be there including their parents, carer, social worker and sometimes a teacher and an interpreter.

If, at the review, the young person doesn't want to say what they feel in front of their parents they can ask for them to leave the room. One of the very important people at the review will be the Independent Reviewing Officer (IRO). They are specifically there to ensure the meeting focuses essentially on the needs of the young person and ensures the young person has their say. See page 10

? What happens before the young person's review?

The young person will be asked, usually to write down points they wish to discuss in advance. This is usually done on a printed form and includes:

- How they are getting on.
- What they want to happen.
- Anything else they would like to talk about at the review.

Their social worker and carer will also be asked to write down what they think as well. Everyone should see what the others have written before the review.

? Will someone take notes of what is said at the meeting?

Yes, the Independent Reviewing Officer (IRO) will make notes and everyone including the young person should get a copy. It is the responsibility of the IRO to ensure the young person is clear about what is being discussed, is happy with the recommendations or where they may not agree, understands why decisions are being made. If a young person disagrees with a matter, encourage them to put their view in writing and try to get the notes changed or re-looked at, at the next meeting.

Help them to follow up matters if what has been agreed doesn't happen within a reasonable amount of time. The time for action to be taken should be agreed at the review.

Disruption meetings: when a placement breaks down

When a placement breaks down a disruption meeting should be called to:
- Help the young person by understanding their needs better.
- Improve practice by understanding what went wrong.
- Recognise all the positive work and good experiences for the young person amongst the difficulties.
- Support everyone and help them to carry on and recover.
- Demonstrate that disruption is never the fault of one or two people, or the result of a single factor. A placement breakdown is invariably the outcome of a whole series of connected factors. The point of having a disruption meeting is to learn from the experience and to develop a more suitable plan for the young person.

? *Who should be present?*

There should always be an independent chairperson, who has not been connected with the placement. Those who should attend include:
- Foster carers, both the current ones and past carers as appropriate.
- Adoptive parents, again as appropriate.
- All social workers who have been involved in the placement.
- Those social workers currently responsible for the child or young person.
- The team manager.
- Someone to take minutes of the meeting.

Agenda for disruption meetings

The following should be considered:
1. The young person's early history before being looked after by the local authority.
2. Care history, before this placement.
3. The assessment and preparation of the young person and the panel decision regarding placement.
4. The assessment and preparation of the applicants, and the panel decision.
5. The matching of the young person and family, and the panel decision.
6. The introductory period where appropriate.
7. The actual placement.
8. What has happened since the placement disrupted.
9. The young person's current priority needs.

Note: *disruption meetings are not planning meetings for the future but they can provide valuable information that can inform planning meetings.*

The report of the disruption meeting should be distributed to everyone who was invited to the meeting. It should only be given to specified people with the agreement of those at the meeting.

The young person's social worker is usually responsible for organising the meeting.

Family group conferences

Family group conferences are meetings set up to assist a family in drawing up a plan for the care of a young person when it may be possible for the young person to remain within their own family. A typical model might be:

1. **Referral**

   Agree the need for a plan. A co-ordinator is appointed who should be matched with the family's race, culture, language and religion.

2. **Stage One**

   The co-ordinator, in consultation with the young person and their immediate carers, identifies the 'family', issues invitations, agrees suitable venues, dates and timing, and prepares the participants.

3. **Stage Two**

   At the start of the meeting the co-ordinator chairs the information-sharing. Professionals explain their roles, responsibilities and concerns and local resources. The family can seek clarification.

4. **Stage Three**

   This is a private planning time for the family when the professionals and co-ordinator withdraw. The family needs to agree a plan, contingency plans and to review arrangements.

5. **Stage Four**

   The co-ordinator and the professionals rejoin the family and hear the plan. Resources are negotiated and the plan agreed unless it places the young person at risk of significant harm.

The meetings should be carefully planned and managed throughout and promises should not be made unless they can be kept and kept within a reasonably agreed timeframe.

Family group conferences enable the young person's family to feel involved and to offer care and support for a young person. Where at all possible and safe, children should be cared for within their family.

Child protection conferences

? *What is a child protection conference?*

This is a meeting that is called if children's services, the police, a teacher, doctor, or anyone else thinks a young person may be suffering, or is at serious risk of suffering, significant harm and may need protection because of:

- physical injury
- neglect
- sexual abuse
- emotional abuse

? *Who goes to a child protection conference?*

Any of the following may attend:

- the young person
- their parents
- their carer if the young person is being looked after
- their social worker and others from the caring services
- the police

- teachers
- a doctor or someone from the health authority
- lawyers representing any of those concerned including the young person or their parents

The young person may also bring along a friend or someone they trust just to be there or to speak on their behalf.

A member of staff from the children's services department or someone independent chairs the meeting and a minute taker will be in attendance.

? Who gets a copy of the minutes?

Everyone present at the meeting or invited will get a copy. If the parents are only present for part of the time they will only be given the minutes of that part of the meeting.

? What happens at the meeting?

The first Child Protection Conference is called to exchange information and to decide on whether the young person should be on a Child Protection Plan. If so, then someone will be nominated to:
- Co-ordinate the plan and this will be monitored by a core group. They will meet regularly, usually on a monthly basis.
- Help the young person and parents to take part in the plan.
- Keep the young person informed of what is going on.

The plan is made to ensure the young person is kept safe and well and that they get any help needed. This is monitored by the core group which will in turn report to the child protection conference review. The plan will also show any other action that may be necessary. Whatever is agreed at the meeting should be carefully explained to the young person.

? What is a core group?

They have the responsibility to ensure that everyone is working together to keep the young person safe. The membership of the core group will have been identified at the child protection conference and must include:
- the key worker, who leads or chairs the core group
- the young person if they are able to understand and take part
- parents and relevant family members
- professionals involved with the young person or parent
- foster carers

? When will the young person no longer need a child protection plan?

- If the plan made at the child protection conference is successful and it is thought that a young person is no longer at risk.
- If the reasons that originally led to the registration no longer apply.
- The young person has moved to another area and that area has accepted responsibility for the case.
- The young person is 18 years old.
- The young person has married.

The first two categories always require a conference to take place. A receiving-in conference should be held when a young person who is the subject of a child protection plan leaves one authority and enters a new one. All other categories may be agreed without the need for a conference.

? *How often do these child protection conferences take place?*

The review conference will usually take place within three months of the initial child protection conference. They must be held at least every six months to review the situation, more often if necessary, until such time as everyone agrees they are no longer required.

For further information, see your child protection procedures. All professionals should be familiar with these procedures and have easy access to them. Different local authorities may involve key workers and carers differently in child protection and post child protection work.

Working with parents

There is an over-riding requirement that contact between a young person who is looked after and their family, and those connected with them, must be encouraged unless it would put the young person in danger or be abusive. As far as possible, carers should work with parents to encourage positive contact. Even if a care order is in force, contact must be encouraged unless the order says otherwise.

Research (confirmed by the Department of Health) has shown that a very large number of young people who are looked after return home again, often quite soon. Keeping contact with families is therefore especially important and it is crucial to make good links with a young person's family within the first weeks of them being looked after. This can determine how often a young person will meet up with the family in the future and would hopefully strengthen positive links.

The young person's social worker should call a meeting with everyone concerned including the young person. This is called a placement planning meeting and should take place before the placement or within a week of it. This meeting needs to clarify, amongst other things, the range and extent of contact for the young person including with extended family members. This can include important friends. The young person should be encouraged to say who they feel are important to them. Some young people may come from a background where those who are not necessarily related to them may be more important to them. Equally, young people who are, for example, asylum-seekers may have quite complicated connections to various adults which will need to be carefully considered. An agreement on delegated authority should also be reached. See page 14.

> *Partnership with families is the most important part. But it can be difficult when one side of the partnership does not want to take into consideration what the young person's wishes are.*
> carer

> *…on the other hand many young people resent the fact that parents who have not bothered about them in the past should suddenly be involved in decision making about their lives.*
> carer

> *When they tell me it's a good idea to see my family, I tell them where to go!*
> young person

Supervised or unsupervised contact

The issue of whether contact arrangements are to be supervised or unsupervised would depend in whether there are any actual or perceived risks to the young person and whether the young person wants the contact to be supervised.

Supervised contact can take place in the foster carer's home when the responsibility for supervision would usually fall on the foster carer or on a responsible adult within the household. However, much supervised contact takes place in contact centres, meeting centres and other designated spaces – sometimes even in restaurants, parks or other play areas.

Unsupervised contact usually takes place when it is clear that there is no risk to the young person and they want it to be that way. It is also very common for young people to move to unsupervised contact as they grow up and are better able to protect themselves and as the original risk to them may have diminished. Unsupervised contact also takes place because young people will vote with their feet and will visit even if it goes against their care plan. Be aware of this and work with the young person's wish to see their family rather than forbid it outright.

How carers can help

- Talk to the young person regularly, about all sorts of things. A young person will probably come round to talking about their family at some time even if they have initially been reluctant.
- Find out all you can; it may be that you should read the young person's file.
- Sometimes a brother, sister, grandparent, relative or friend can act as a go-between.
- Take things slowly, one step at a time – don't rush.
- If you arrange a first meeting, make it on neutral ground.
- If either party refuses to make contact at first, don't give up, but be sensitive to the difficulties.
- Develop good relations with the young person's family or friends and listen to what they have to say.

There may be lots of anger or hurt: explain things as you see them to both sides. There may also be feelings of guilt – young people often mistakenly think 'it's my fault'. Most young people really do want contact with parents even if they won't admit it or are very angry with them.

The following are just two quotes, one from a girl and the other from a boy:

…We should try hard to stick with our families.

…At the end of the day everyone has to have contact with their family.

Encouraging contact with families

There are practical things that you could do to encourage young people to keep in contact with their family:

- When the young person comes to your home, get them to bring their own duvet or other items from their bedroom if possible. It may help them feel more secure and it will remind them of their home and their family. The smell may also be comforting.

- Use creative ways of keeping parents involved and informed.
- The parents could be involved with holidays, outings with school, with health check ups etc.
- Suggest that parents have contact in your home – if the local authority (or court) agrees and there is no risk involved.
- Once good contact is established, parents could be asked to come to the home to help out in a practical way such as cooking, organising a visit or demonstrating a particular skill they may have.
- For more independent young people, suggest they visit their parents at home for a short while, gradually building up to an overnight stay, then a weekend visit – if the local authority (or court) agrees and the young person will be safe. This contact needs to form part of the young person's overall plan.

Keeping parents in touch with what is going on in the young person's life makes it much easier for parents to work in partnership. The young person may be in touch with, or willing to see, other family members such as grandparents or aunts and uncles. This should be encouraged (providing the court and local authority agree) as it is a good way to maintain family links and it may lead to better contact with parents in the future.

Once you have got the contact going, you will have to help to keep it going. You will probably also have to explain to both parties:
- Just what 'working in partnership' means in practice.
- What the benefits are for both sides.
- That talking and discussing are better than arguing and shouting.
- That it's better to work together to help the young person move into adulthood.

However, if it really won't work out, have a plan ready so you know how you will handle the situation from both sides.

There may be other important people in a young person's life with whom they may need help to keep in touch.

Of course there will be setbacks, these are only to be expected. Act as a mediator, if you can, by:
- Helping the young person to remember family birthdays.
- Inviting families to special events.
- Encouraging telephone contact, texts and emails.
- Encouraging the exchange of photographs.
- Being welcoming when families come.
- Telling parents that their travelling expenses may be paid.
- Sharing information.

It is a requirement that you keep a record of whenever contact is made between families and the young person.

How to manage contact when things may not work out

Unfortunately, some parents may not wish to co-operate with the authorities and the foster carer even if they are told it will be in the interests of their child if they do. Managing contact under these circumstances will be extremely challenging, especially given the increase and ease of use of mobile phones and email. BAAF and The Fostering Network have both produced useful information on this. It is important that you work closely with the young person's social worker and others to ensure that the impact of uncooperative parents are minimised.

Remember: most young people will return to their birth family once they have left care and many will be visiting or meeting with them whilst they are still looked after. This reality needs to be borne in mind when considering what action needs to be taken.

Young carers

Young carers usually spend a lot of their time, energy and emotions caring for a parent who has serious health needs. Usually young carers are living at home with their parents, looking after them as well as any younger siblings they may have. Be sensitive to the needs of such young people if they are placed into your family, particularly if they have been placed because their parent has become critically ill or has died. There are support groups as well as useful literature which might help you support and care for these young people.

Unaccompanied Asylum Seekers and Refugee Children (UASRC)

The way USARC come into the country and become known to children's services means that most of their placements start out being unplanned emergency placements.

A foster carer who has a UASRC placement should be clear about what such placements entail. At the initial stage the task might be to provide a home while an assessment of the young person's needs is being carried out. However a placement often continues after assessment. A foster carer will need to understand the impact on a young person who:

- Has little or no contact with their family of origin.
- Is new to the country.
- Is frightened or confused about what is going to happen to them and also to their family.
- Does not speak English or only has a very limited vocabulary.
- Is traumatised by their previous experiences.

Carers may also be supported by professionals who are working within ever changing policies in their work. Carers are at the forefront of the young person's struggle to deal with the impact of their past experiences, their integration of the present and the realities of the future. So that these young people can be helped, it is important for carers to find out as much as possible about:

- the young person
- their background and cultural history
- any known plans
- what the young person's expectations are for the future

Many young people who are considered to be unaccompanied asylum seekers or refugee young people do not want to discuss, or are unable to discuss, their past. They may have been warned not to and think if they did so it would jeopardise further their security in the UK.

Some young people may in reality be older than they have stated as they may have lowered their stated age because they are fearful of being deported. The Home Office has devised an assessment method aimed at checking this. It is likely that if you care for a young person in these circumstances they will be required to be assessed.

This is a very skilled task as carers have to prepare the young person for two potential futures – one in the UK and the other back in their country of origin as the decision regarding a young person's stay is often not taken until the young person is nearing their 18th birthday. Help and advice should be sought from a wide variety of sources including other people from similar backgrounds if at all possible.

The children of foster carers

There will be times when your own children will get on with foster children but also times they will not, but it is essential to have the commitment of the whole family when you are fostering. You need to be honest with your children and make time where you regularly discuss how you and they are all feeling. The honesty should include:
- What the future will be like, and how some things will have to change.
- What to expect of the young person.

Your children may find adjusting to being part of a foster family hard and may wish you to stop. It is important that you are able to discuss this with your fostering agency or SSW. They are responsible for trying to ensure your own children are not upset by the fostering experience. Resources are available to help your children to understand or cope with what is going on.

Your children should be seen regularly by your SSW and should be encouraged and invited to contribute to the foster care annual review. No one will be expecting your children's views of fostering to be uncritical. Just like you, they will have good and bad experiences. The important thing is that they are being heard and have the opportunity to be supported and helped. Ultimately, however, if your children really are not coping with fostering or they are going through a particularly difficult period, you may be asked to stop fostering for a while. This is only likely in extreme situations but would, nevertheless, be in line with their duty towards your children as well as the foster children.

Many people have fixed ideas and still regard foster children as problem children – there is still a stigma. Young people of foster carers need to be given:
- Facts and information about fostering.
- A few stock answers to awkward questions – 'don't be nosy' might be what they want to say but daren't and developing a cover story may be useful. See page 26.

Foster carer's children also need to know that:
- They have rights as members of a family.
- They will be listened to.
- That their parents will be open and frank with them.
- That they should be open and frank with their parents.

Carers and their children could perhaps draw up an informal contract with agreed rules for **all** on:

- Acceptable language ie how to talk about some issues.
- Meals and meal times.
- Bed times.
- Coming-in times.
- Pocket money.
- Home rules, such as if a young person gets up in the night, should they flush the toilet.

A young person needs to know that some of the house rules or the safer caring rules are meant to prevent them from being uncomfortable or embarrassed. Don't bombard the young person with them. Tell them the important things first and you can tell them about the rest at a later stage. Think of easy and creative ways of getting the message across.

In some regions, groups have been set up for the children of foster carers. Some independent foster agencies seem particularly good at involving foster carers' children in the fostering process and local authorities should learn from this practice. More needs to be done to ensure that the voice of the children of foster carers is heard.

Problems should not be allowed to stew.
Now is the best time to talk if there is a problem or worry.

House rules and safer caring

House rules are about ensuring everyone in the household understands how to keep safe and comfortable. These rules may take into account religious or cultural beliefs, for example – no outside shoes worn in the house.

Your agency will usually give you basic safer caring guidelines but these will need to be adapted to the particular circumstances of your household and the needs of the children placed with your family

When drawing up safer caring or house-rules, you should be looking at how to manage risk. For example, most young people would know that knives are kept in the kitchen and would not think to use them as a weapon. It is not possible for young people to be kept completely risk-free in a home but it is important that you consider what might be a risk to each young person. In any event, the house rules, as with your safer caring rules, should be reviewed regularly.

Remember a foster home is a home like any other and young people are living with risks all the time. It is important that young people learn to keep themselves safe.

Cover stories

Developing a cover story helps to offer explanations about a fostered young person without having to reveal sensitive matters. Cover stories should be kept simple. The whole of your extended family network will not need to know everything about the young person in your care but they should be told enough to enable everyone to feel confident and comfortable.

Cover stories are also a means of helping the young person to discuss their situation, for example with their friends or at school. The same cover story should be used by your own children and this should help them to respond to questions.

It will be relatively obvious that a young person, who is not your own, has come to stay and that this will arouse curiosity and interest. Some people may already know that you are a foster carer. However, unless there is a reason for someone to know anything more than just the fact that the young person has come to stay, then they should not be told.

Basically:
- Tell the person asking, that the young person cannot live with their own parents at the moment and that they have come to live with you.
- Ask them to respect the fact that you cannot talk about this with them any further and that you hope that the young person can be accepted as part of your family.
- Explain that no one should be deliberately asking the young person questions about their family or situation.

Help the young person develop and practise the cover story. If they are asked 'where are your parents?' they should say, in their own way, 'they cannot look after me at the moment so I am living with…' This will mean that if their parents are in prison, for example, they will not have to tell anyone.

The social workers should provide those who will need to know more about the fostered young person, for example the new school, with the necessary information about their previous education and other relevant facts. There should be a clear agreement with the school about how they manage this information as foster children should not be made a scapegoat, or be bullied or singled out or made to feel in any way different.

A welcome book

When a young person first comes into your home they may be bewildered, scared or angry. Get your own children to think of something welcoming that you can all do together. Also ensure that you have a welcome book which you could give to the young person to keep, not only to refer to, but also they may wish to add this to their own life book.

The welcome book could include:
- Pictures and details about you and your family and your extended network. The latter would be important for the young person to know as they will be able to identify other people who they may see regularly and who may be involved with them.
- Pictures and details of your house and any rules there may be about the rooms – e.g. that no-one is allowed into anyone else's room without permission (including the foster child's).
- Information about pets, hobbies and what your family like to do.
- Any routines or expectations there are in the household.
- What to do in case of an emergency such as a fire.

Think of all the information that a young person might need. Put it in a fun but clear way to help them to settle in and feel secure. You will also need to tell them what the rules are about the use of mobile phones, the Internet and other technologies

Collecting mementos and compiling a life book

Talking about their past is often a very painful experience for young people and many don't want to do it. All young people have a past, a present, and a future. Wait until the time is right to talk about where they have lived, who they have lived with, what memories they have and what more they would like to know. Keeping mementos is a way of filling in the jigsaw of a young person's life, both in the past and for the future.

They may bring with them mementos that are important to them, or they may bring nothing, hoping to wipe out bad memories. What is a treasure to one young person may be trash to another but is it important for young people to be helped to realise the importance of some things and how some things may be irreplaceable.

You could encourage a young person to have an envelope or a box handy where you or they can stick their mementos or photos and keep them safe. It's also worth keeping a good filing system of photographs taken, as it can be disappointing for the young person when they decide they want to remember a particular event and the photographs can't be found! This is relatively easily done on a computer and it is also easy to scan in old pictures.

Ensure that young people leave their placement with positive memories. Some young people may wish to do some life work (sometimes known as life story work) and the following explains this in more detail.

Life work

Life work (sometimes known as 'life story work') is a way of giving young people a chance to learn about their past life and history. It should help them to understand some of the things that have happened. Often the information is put together safely into an album which may be called a life book but can equally be done on computer. There are a number of useful books, for instance, *The New Life Work Model* (Nicholls, 2005) with its accompanying workbook *My Memory Book 8+*. There are also CDs and other ways which can help the young person and guide the person working with them on this task.

But I know all about me!
- A young person might think they do but often their memory, or what they have been told, is not correct.
- Will they remember when they are an adult?
- Who will be around to tell them?

Some information will be on files kept by the young person's local authority but things like photographs and keepsakes need to be put together whilst they can still be found. Sadly though, information sometimes just cannot be found.

? *How long will it take to do?*

That depends on whoever is doing life work with the young person – but it might be once a week for say an hour or two over a few months. It depends on whether they will be going out to take photographs, make visits or whether it is just a question of organising what is already there.

Some ideas for life work:
- drawing family trees
- tracing maps of places of importance to the young person
- putting photographs into an album
- writing down memories after a chat
- visiting cemeteries to look at gravestones

It all depends on how much the young person wants to include or how much research they want to do.

? *Must the young person do it?*

Everyone has a right to privacy so, of course, the answer is 'no', but many young people who have left care say they wish they had done it. Although at times painful and difficult for a young person, the process of making the life book helps them to understand their past. They will know things about themselves which they will be able to share with their own family and friends either now or in the future.

? *Whose book is it?*

It belongs to the young person but you may offer to keep it in a safe place as photographs and keepsakes may not easily be replaced. But it really is up to the young person what they do with it and to whom they show it. It is also a good idea to add to it with photographs and mementos of the young person's time with you. As far as possible do two life books or keep a copy on a computer or memory stick as it is common for young people who are angry to destroy their original book and then regret this much later.

Complaints

Young people who are old enough and want to make a complaint may need a lot of help to do so and making a complaint should be seen as a positive step. It means the young person has:
- Thought about the situation.
- Decided that something is not right.
- Is willing to do something about it.

Foster homes and children's homes that encourage criticism and comment will be better places in which to live. It is healthy and necessary for moans to be discussed openly and for everyone's point of view heard. One children's home manager said: *'We've only had 10 complaints this month.'* She was disappointed, as she had tried to encourage more. She saw complaints from young people as a way of improving the care and service provided and of making the home a better place for the young people to live.

This section does not deal with **allegations of abuse** as such allegations should be dealt with through the safeguarding of children procedures. Whilst ultimately, they may result in a complaint being made, they follow a very different path. These are discussed within Section 2.

Generally there are two different types of complaints.
1. The really serious ones which must be handled directly through the complaints procedures.

2. Those which can be handled within the home, such as moans, suggestions and problems – like the ones the manager above was referring to. Complaints of this nature will happen in any family home.

What may seem unimportant to you may be very serious to a young person. Similarly, something a young person has learned to put up with, such as harassment, discrimination or bullying are extremely serious and should be investigated. Young people may feel that it is not worth making a complaint, for example against their social worker, either because they might be victimised or because they think the system is stacked against them. It is important that young people are helped and encouraged should they wish to complain.

If a formal complaint is made, an investigating officer will be appointed as well as someone from the local authority management team. Separately, each will carry out an investigation. The young person should be kept informed of what is going on by those investigating. They should be informed of the outcome of the complaint.

Harassment and discrimination

Complaints about sexual or racial harassment or racial discrimination must be taken seriously. Carers may not feel able to help a young person in some circumstances for all sorts of reasons. If this is the case, you should put them in touch with someone who can. These might be:
- senior members of staff
- citizens advice bureau
- local councillors
- ombudsmen
- the local authority complaints offers
- one of the many free helplines or children's rights organisations
- the courts – young people can ask for a judicial review (over a legal matter)

Some hints for handling a formal complaint
- Ask the young person what they would like to see done about the complaint.
- Listen to the young person's complaint. Make sure you fully understand it, and take notes. Give the young person a copy of the notes, let them check the facts and details before any further action is taken.
- Ensure the young person understands that there are other people they can go to for support if they do not wish to disclose all the complaint to you.
- Don't make your own judgements about the complaint but help them to understand that making a complaint also involves a sense of responsibility. They should be helped to clarify the rights and wrongs of taking such action.
- Agree a way forward and enable the young person to be involved in the process as much as possible, for instance by making contact themselves with the authority's complaint's section.
- Understand the way the complaints process will work as you will need to keep reminding the young person about it.

Some hints for handling other complaints

- Listen attentively to the young person's complaint. Make sure you fully understand it. Take notes.
- Show that you understand their feelings and praise them for raising the matter.
- State your own position undefensively and without hostility.
- Find out if the young person has any suggestions for resolving the complaint.
- If appropriate, say that you will do your best to correct the situation and make suggestions such as holding a family meeting or involving the young person's social worker.
- Review the safer caring or house rules as necessary.
- Always set clear follow-up dates and provide a copy of your notes if the young person is old enough to understand.

Discrimination

The dictionary definition of discrimination is: 'to treat differently because of prejudice'.

Many different people are discriminated against for a wide variety of reasons. Because they are:

- fat
- in care
- old
- have different ways of doing things
- young
- work hard at school
- female
- don't like sport
- gay
- disabled
- white, in an area where there are mainly black people
- black, in an area where there are mainly white people

> **Discrimination of all kinds is wrong. Discrimination is offensive.**

? *What are the main types of discrimination?*

Direct discrimination

Direct discrimination happens when you are treated worse than others or segregated from them, because of your race, colour, nationality, or ethnic or national origin, disability, sex or sexual orientation.

Indirect discrimination

This is more complicated. It happens when everyone seems to be treated in the same way, but, in practice, people from a certain group are put at a greater disadvantage. The law says that when a rule hits a particular group harder than others (intentionally or not) and there's no good reason for the rule – it is still discrimination.

Victimisation

If you are victimised because you have complained about discrimination, or because you have supported someone else's complaint, this, too, is unlawful discrimination.

Discrimination applies to:
- jobs
- training
- housing
- education
- services – from councils, banks, insurance companies, pubs, clubs, discos, restaurants, cinemas, travel agencies and so on.

It is important to realise that some people are discriminated against in more than one of these ways, falling into more than one of the groups which suffer discrimination, for example, they may be black and disabled.

Why do people discriminate?

Some people discriminate because they do not like a particular group or situation. Many people discriminate without realising it.

Discrimination doesn't just mean treating someone differently, it also includes using names, or words, no matter how innocently, which put people down. If you hear name calling going on, ensure you discuss it. All too often young people don't realise how hurtful and cruel they are being. Young people may not understand what the words they are using really mean. It may be something they have heard others say.

Am I black or am I white?

'Am I black or am I white?
I used to ask that question
every day and night
why do you ask a question
as obvious as that?

It's plain to see that you are black
But being in care
In a white community
It's hard to decide
with no black family'

These are the first two verses of a poem by Margaret Parr in *Black Experiences of Improving Practice with Children and Families*. It highlights the problems of a black young person being cared for by white carers.

? What does the law say?

The law says that careful consideration should be made to the young person's religious persuasion, racial origin, cultural and linguistic background. Where young people are disabled the local authority must provide services to help the disabled young person to lead the lives they wish.

Recognising differences

Differences should not be ignored. People are not all the same. Some people have different skin colour, hair, religious backgrounds. They may practise different rites in relation to their culture. Some young people have different languages. Some young people may be in a wheelchair or have a speech impediment.

Respecting differences

No one should be discriminated against because of their difference. Young people may need your help to learn to respect differences whilst other young people will need extra support or resources to help live as full a life as possible.

Meeting racial, disability, religious, cultural, dietary and cosmetic needs

Young people may previously have been living with their own birth families or have been looked after away from their families. As their carer, you will need to find out what the young person has been used to and what practices they would like to follow. The young person may have strong views on whether or not they want for example to eat Asian or Caribbean food; attend a Mosque or Church; wear their hair in a particular way; be treated differently because of their disability.

Young people may:
- Want to know where to buy certain foods or cream for their hair or skin.
- Need to buy braille materials or find out how to get access to different places if they are in a wheelchair.
- Need support and help to explore different possibilities for their life.
- Need to feel confident about asking for and getting specialist help.

Colour and language

The language we use to describe ourselves and others can be very important in establishing self confidence and identity. In the UK at present, the term 'Black' is often used to cover a wide group of people from different origins However, some people do not like this collective term and prefer their individual nationality to be used, e.g. Chinese, Asian. The term 'Black' has been used by some as a political term of unity. You may feel it appropriate to discuss this with the young person in your care.

If you feel you need any more information about looking after young people from cultural backgrounds different from your own, you may find it helpful to refer to a book published by the National Children's Bureau, *Religion, Ethnicity, Sex Education – Exploring the Issues*, which highlights the importance of understanding different cultural norms, such as those regarding puberty, circumcision etc. In Section 7 there are some very brief notes on some of the more common religions practised in the UK.

Building pride and esteem

All young people need positive images of themselves, their background and way of life. Carers can help by:
- Building pride and esteem by showing the young person that they have capabilities, talents and potential.
- Finding out all you can about the background, history and culture of any young person who lives with you. It may be something you could do together. The internet is a good starting point for this research.

- Discussing with the young person and parents what food the young person likes to eat and then discover together the shops that sell such foods.
- Asking the parents or find out the names and addresses of local youth groups where young people can meet other young people of their own culture or religion or other disabled young people if they wish.
- Giving support. Young people will need help and guidance in all sorts of ways, for example, on how to complain and to whom to complain.

Carers' support groups could discuss discrimination and carers could help each other with practical suggestions on how they coped with past situations such as racist neighbours or name calling by other young people. Carers should also challenge discrimination about being in care.

Carers should also think very carefully before taking responsibility for a young person from a different culture if they think they will be unable to promote their welfare.

Disability

The following advice and suggestions are given on terms to use and avoid when working with young people with disabilities, and also for helping young people who may have someone with a disability living in the same home:

- Do offer help, but don't get upset if it is rejected – sometimes it will be welcome, but sometimes it won't be needed or may hinder the disabled person doing it in their own, possibly slower but effective way.
- Young people may become angry or aggressive as they try to come to terms with their disability or want to learn to become independent. Be aware and quietly understanding.
- Do not make assumptions.
- Don't make comments like 'I don't know how you manage' or 'I'd die if I was blind/deaf/couldn't walk'.
- Speak directly to the person, not to whoever may be with them. People still say 'Does he take sugar?'
- Find out about the young person's special needs or disability as soon as possible.
- Have high but realistic expectations of the young person.
- Stress the good things.
- Praise, reassure.
- Encourage the young person to take part in a wide variety of activities.
- Help/teach them to play, find activities they can do individually, with groups in similar situations and with all young people.
- Help the young person to mix with others.
- Don't treat them differently but as individuals.
- Talk to them, discuss and explain.
- As with other young people, sometimes young people with disabilities need firm boundaries. Set them. Equally disabled young people will have the same needs as other young people but may need more sensitive help, for instance in helping them to understand their developing sexual needs.
- Be patient.

Section 4

A Place to Live

Before a young person is looked after there should have been a placement planning meeting where arrangements are discussed and clarified. The aim in most, but not all, cases will be to get a young person back living with their parents or guardians as soon as possible.

Wherever they live, young people need to know what to expect and what the rules of the house are. It would be good to have a welcome book (see page 27) containing useful information about where they are going to live and about the people living there to give the young person when they arrive.

Foster homes

? *Being fostered, what does is mean?*

It means a young person (and hopefully their brothers and sisters) will be looked after by a foster carer in the foster carer's home. This may be either for a short time while things are sorted out at home or for a longer period, depending on the situation.

? *Can anyone be a foster carer?*

No, anyone can apply, but all applicants are carefully vetted.

? *What happens?*

Once the young person is fostered, their local authority will try to find a foster carer who is suitable, i.e. someone who, as far as possible:

- Has the same background and racial origin.
- Has the same religion (if they have one).
- Understands their needs.
- Lives close by so they can attend the same school.
- Has other children in their family or does not have any children depending on the young person's needs.

Although not always possible, the local authority should enable the young person to visit the carer's house, in advance. The young person and the carer will then decide if they want to carry on. Once this is agreed the local authority will make all the necessary arrangements. Their social worker should visit regularly to review the arrangements.

If the foster family is from a different racial background the social worker, or whoever is responsible, will try to ensure the young person has contact with people of similar background and opportunities to keep in touch if the young person wants this.

Although every care is taken to make a young person's stay with a foster family successful, sometimes it just does not work out. This may be through no fault of anyone: circumstances may change.

Children's homes

These are houses of varying sizes that provide young people who cannot live at home with the best possible quality of life in the circumstances. They are run by local authorities or organisations such as Barnardo's or Catholic Children's Homes with a team of staff, usually led by a manager. Staff will be on duty on a rota basis 24 hours a day, 365 days a year.

Sometimes the home will be separated into sections so that part of it will be made into small flats, often called independent units where young people can learn skills such as budgeting and cooking to help them prepare for when they are no longer 'looked after'. Sometimes their stay will be short lived and they can go back to living with their parents or they may be helped to move into a place of their own.

A key worker from the children's home is normally allocated to each young person but the young person will still have their social worker. If this is not the case then the key worker may be asked to undertake some social work duties such as acting as advocate for the young person on a temporary basis.

The young person will be encouraged to attend school, college or work regularly, to bring friends to the home and to act responsibly around the house: the house rules are often set in partnership with the young people.

Supported lodgings

This is where a young person can live with a family or within a household that can keep an eye on them and help them to learn the necessary skills and gain the necessary confidence before they can move into accommodation of their own. A person in the household will have been assessed and considered suitable to help the young person in their route towards adult life. It is very difficult and can be scary coming out of care and supported lodgings offers a safe place from which to take the next step.

Families or households who offer supported lodgings are paid to offer a secure base and offer advice and guidance like a very friendly, helpful and caring landlord.

Secure units

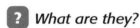 *What are they?*

Secure units are for young people whose liberty needs to be restricted due to a criminal activity including being a risk to others. Some secure accommodation will be attached to a children's home: others will be located separately. It may be necessary for a young person to be housed in secure accommodation outside their area if there are no facilities or vacancies locally.

No-one under the age of 13 years may be placed in secure accommodation without the permission of the Secretary of State, nor can they be kept in a secure unit for more than 72 hours over any one period of 28 days without a court order.

? *When might I be sent to a secure unit?*

There are very strict regulations on when a young person's liberty can be restricted. If the young person has not committed an offence a young person should only be placed in secure accommodation if:

- They have a history of absconding and are likely to abscond from any other type of accommodation; and if, when they abscond, they are likely to suffer significant harm.
- If the young person is kept in any other type of accommodation they are likely to injure themselves or other people.

The court has the power to send young offenders to secure accommodation in certain circumstances. A young person placed in secure accommodation will have all normal rights except freedom to leave the building.

The home environment

The environment in which we all live is really important, much more important than many realise. A young person said that although the staff seemed nicer at a particular residential home, she said she wouldn't go there because 'It was a mess – how could I take my friends to a place like that?'

It is important to involve young people in how the home is organised and decorated, as this will help them establish a sense of belonging and to enjoy being there.

? *What can I do around the house?*

Involve young people in:

- Choosing colour schemes.
- Actually decorating, not just their room but other parts of the house.
- Choosing any new furniture, equipment or pictures.
- Changing the layout of different parts of the house.
- Taking responsibility for the care and cleaning of the house or just their room.

? *What can I do in my room?*

They should have their own room: if that's not possible their own space in an agreed part of a room where they can put up pictures, posters etc.

- Let them be responsible for keeping it clean and tidy.
- If they are sharing, let them agree the ground rules with the other occupant.
- Give them a key to their room: only go in their room when they are not there if it is essential.
- Young people with a disability should be helped to live a full life: you may have to make changes around the home.

If something gets broken or damaged, don't just leave it or call in the expert to do the job. If possible, work with the young person who caused the damage or any others interested in putting it right. They may respect it more next time.

A few indoor plants here and there will give a good feeling to a home – possibly grown by the young people, and certainly nurtured by them. Let them cut the grass or hoe the flowerbeds.

Not only will they be learning life skills but will get the satisfaction from a job well done and be able to admire the results of their efforts.

If food is set out with care it seems to taste much better. If you set standards, many young people will learn what is possible and remember it for the future.

Everyone, whether male or female, should try to make that little extra effort with the way they look. Set an example. The young people will notice. They may laugh at you or compliment you but they will notice. You'll set a standard for them to follow.

It is all part of building up their confidence, making them feel important and making them feel they are taking part in decisions about their lives.

Section 5
Health – Physical and Mental Well-being

Introduction

This section is based on advice received from senior health officials. It is in 2 parts, Staying healthy and Health matters. The second part is in alphabetical order.

Good health is not just about the absence of disease: it is about the overall physical, emotional, and sexual well-being of the young person (emotional health is the term now used, rather than 'mental health'). As such it is totally linked to the overall development of the young person. When we think about health we should also think about healthy living and lifestyles and engagement in cultural and leisure activities.

All young people, when they enter care, should have an initial statutory health needs assessment normally carried out by a doctor, paediatrician, school nurse or designated LAC nurse. This is an opportunity to clarify the young person's past and present health.

Good health is important to everyone. Gradually, young people must have the opportunity to learn to take responsibility for their own health.

Good health is important because:
- If young people are ill or have an accident they'll get better more quickly.
- They'll probably get ill less often anyway.
- They'll be better able to cope with stress.
- They'll have less time off school or work so they'll make better progress.

For looked after children it is particularly important because:
- They have often experienced neglect prior to care.
- Their physical and emotional health is often poor in comparison to their non looked after peers
- They may have a higher level of emotional health needs than their peers

We have not attempted to cover everything in the health section but have tried to give a few pointers, hints and suggestions. School nurses, a designated nurse, looked after children's health teams and GPs will be pleased to help. When a young person is first looked after a carer may need to know:
- What illnesses has the young person had?
- What medication the young person is taking – what quantities and at what intervals?
- What immunisations has the young person had?
- Has the young person been in contact recently with anyone who is infectious?
- Does the young person have any allergies?
- Does the young person have any particular health or dietary needs?
- Are there any family illnesses which it is important to know about, such as a heart condition, diabetes or sight problems?
- Does the young person have any physical impairment?

In some cases the young person may have a particular illness, such as diabetes, and the carer will need specialist advice and training before the young person can live in the carer's home. The above information may be kept on a health record sheet similar to the one shown on pages 61 and 62 or on the parent's own record of their young person's health if you have been given one.

Young people in care should:
- Feel safe, feel respected and be supported in a committed relationship with at least one carer.
- Have access to effective health care, information, treatment and services.
- Have opportunities to develop personal and social skills, and be encouraged to develop their talents, abilities and life skills.
- Be supported to leave, care and provide for themselves.

Staying healthy

Exercise

Everyone needs exercise because it will help improve stamina, strength and overall fitness: it will help their heart and lungs to work better, stop flabby muscles, keep weight down and generally help them cope with life better. It also promotes emotional health and well-being and helps young people to feel good about themselves.

Sleep

No two people need exactly the same amount of sleep but regular sleep is essential. Get young people to work out what's best for them and seek advice from health professionals if you are concerned about sleep patterns and possible sleep disorders.

Diet

This doesn't just mean losing weight. It means thinking about what they eat, how much they eat and why they need certain foods.

Examples of foods that are good are fresh fruit and vegetables, pasta, wholemeal bread, low fat milk, unsaturated margarine, white meat, fish.

Some foods that are not very good are crisps, chocolate, sweets, cakes, fizzy drinks.

It's not as bad as it sounds! Together you can experiment with different recipes. The 'not so good' foods are not of course forbidden, but it is a good idea to cut down on the amount of these a young person eats and drinks. It is also a good idea to grill food instead of frying it and to reduce the amount of sugar and salt a young person eats. See: www.eatwell.gov.uk

If a young person is, or wishes to become, a vegetarian care has to be taken to ensure a balanced diet. The Vegetarian Society www.vegsoc.org or your GP will give details.

Weight

Find out what a young person's ideal weight is and try to get them to stay somewhere near that – sometimes easier said than done! A doctor or nurse will tell them what their weight should be, and weighing machines in chemists shops usually have a chart.

Health matters

Advice and confidentiality

Sometimes young people find it easier to talk to outsiders about health matters. For free and confidential advice they can go to:

- their local doctor
- the school or college nurse if there is one, looked after children's nurse
- youth counsellor with responsibility for health
- contraceptive and sexual health services
- key worker
- independent visitor

Alcohol

Looked after children are four times more likely than their peers to smoke, use alcohol and misuse drugs.

Alcohol is a drug and, as with all drugs, if it is not used sensibly it can cause problems. Drinking too much alcohol can damage health.

Try to persuade young people not to drink heavily just because other people do. It won't make them look big: they will look just the opposite if they have too much – and they'll feel terrible the next day. Drinking alcohol is often linked to peer pressure, life experiences, abuse or low self-esteem so this kind of advice wont always help. Try unpicking the reasons behind their behaviour and find support, counselling or therapy if you feel you can't help. It is also about setting boundaries, helping them find a structure to their life and providing a loving, caring environment.

They may also do things you and they wish they hadn't when they've been drinking alcohol. This could be another topic for discussion.

The following drinks each contain one unit of alcohol:

- 1 single pub measure of spirits
- 1 single glass of sherry or fortified wine
- 1 small glass of table wine
- ½ pint of ordinary lager, beer or cider
- ¼ pint of strong lager, beer or cider

Bicardi Breezers contain 1½ units and spirit mixers even more.

As a rough guide a man should not drink more than 21 units a week and a woman no more than 14 units a week. It is best if young people drink much less than this because alcohol is more likely to be harmful while they are still growing.

If a young person does come home drunk:

- Try to keep them quiet so they don't disturb the rest of the house (easier said than done!). They may also be embarrassed the next morning so would prefer as few people as possible to know.

- If they want to talk, listen.
- If they want a drink, give them water or a cup of tea and sit with them.
- If they want to lay down, take them to their room. Wait until they are in bed. Turn them on their side so they don't inhale any vomit. Give them a bowl to be sick into. Before you leave them, let them know they can call you at any time.

Talk to them later about the dangers of alcohol.

There is a legal age whereby young person can buy alcohol though no actual legal age for when they can drink.

Foster carers should act as role models so the young person can see that sensible drinking can be enjoyable without all the consequences that occur when too much alcohol is drunk.

Allergies

Allergy is an abnormal reaction by the body to substances, often harmless to other people, which are breathed in, swallowed, injected or come into contact with the skin. Allergy to food seems to be on the increase with the use of additives in food. Allergies should be diagnosed with caution under medically controlled conditions. Young people need a balanced diet. Removal of foodstuffs from a young person's diet on shaky evidence of allergy should only be a short-term solution. Every effort should be made to establish the extent of the allergic response.

Many of these conditions may appear worse in times of stress.

Anaphylaxis is an extreme allergic reaction that anyone can have to any allergen. It is still quite rare, but the most common reactions are to peanuts (and some other nuts), wasp and bee stings and different medicines. If you suspect a young person may be at risk of having a severe reaction get their GP to refer them to a hospital consultant. The young person will probably be prescribed an Epi-pen. This is a pre-loaded syringe of adrenaline, which temporarily reduces the allergic reaction. Any young person who is injected should still attend hospital via an emergency ambulance in order to receive further treatment. Carers, parents and school staff will all need training on the administration of the Epi-pen, either through the school nurse or the designated health professional for looked after young people.

Asthma

This is now, by far the most common chronic illness in childhood affecting one in seven children in the UK. Spasm of the small tubes in the lungs makes it difficult to breathe. It shows itself by irregular bouts of coughing, sneezing and breathlessness. Asthma attacks are usually brought on by contact with pollens, feathers, fur (furry pets like dogs, cats, rabbits and hamsters) house dust and house mites. A major trigger for an attack is cigarette smoke. Other factors may be chest infections and colds, vigorous exercise, emotional upsets, stress, sudden changes in temperature and, on rare occasions, laughter.

Treatment for asthma is very good and most young people are able to lead a normal life and attend school regularly. If young people cough at night, wheeze or cannot fully participate in sport they are not being treated correctly and should go back to their GP or to the hospital asthma clinic.

The aim of treatment is to be symptom free. It is most important that preventative inhalers (often inhaled steroid) are taken regularly and consistently. Don't let them make the mistake of stopping using them because the symptoms have gone away. A young person should only stop taking medication on medical advice. Often an asthma (practice) nurse based at the local GP surgery will help and advise young people who have asthma.

Brain development

Adolescence is not only a time of rapid physical change but the brain also changes. Research is starting to demonstrate how changes in the brain structure and the way it works responds to the way a young person is changing. There is evidence that the brain continues to develop until the mid-20s, especially our decision-making skills. This is significant when we consider the age when the average birth child leaves home compared to the age a young person who has been in foster care is expected to set up on their own.

Dental care

Teeth can last a lifetime if they are looked after well.
- Tooth decay is avoidable.
- Encourage young people to restrict foods and drinks containing sugar to mealtimes.
- If they are thirsty between meals, suggest they drink water or milk, though water is the best and is the only drink they should have during the night.
- If it is necessary for the young person to take medicine make sure it is a 'sugar free' one. If not available, a young person should rinse their teeth and gums after taking the medicine.
- Teeth should be brushed daily at night and at one other time.

Young people often have very little sense of the amount of time that they should clean their teeth. Get them to sing or hum a favourite tune in their head – this should last about two minutes and will give them a good guide as to the length of time teeth need to be cleaned. Alternatively a kitchen timer or alarm clock might be helpful.

Fluoride helps to make teeth strong.

Visiting the dentist

To find a dentist use the search facility on any NHS Choices page. Encourage young people to get into the habit of regular check-ups as this should help prevent any decay or gum problems.

Ideas for between-meal snacks if these are really necessary:
- Peeled and chopped fruit and vegetables.
- Dairy foods such as cubes of cheese or plain yoghurt or fromage frais – added fruit helps too.
- Plain biscuits such as water biscuits, crispbreads or Melba toast.
- Sandwiches, rolls or wraps filled with lean meat, fish, cheese spread, grated cheese or egg. Salad vegetables could also be added.
- Any type of bread including toasted fingers, chapattie, pitta bread, potato cakes, matzos and savoury scones.

Toothpaste

- Look on the packet or tube for the amount of fluoride in the toothpaste and choose one containing 1350-1500 ppm ('ppm' stands for 'parts per million').
- After brushing, spit out but do not rinse out – this allows the fluoride in the toothpaste to stay on the teeth longer

Young people should also work with you to ensure they eat a healthy diet. When out shopping read food labels together to discover whether a product contains sugar. Watch out for sugar under different names such as glucose, glucose syrup, sucrose, dextrose, fructose and maltose. Acidic drinks such as undiluted pure fruit juice, fizzy drinks and squash can damage teeth. Encourage young people to learn to do this automatically for themselves.

Appliance treatment

Wearing a brace for example – encourage the young person to be responsible both for wearing their own brace and for ensuring it is kept hygienically clean. Orthodontic treatment is only free for children up to the age of 18, or 19 if they are in full time education as long as there is a clinical need. It is not free purely for cosmetic reasons

Teeth whitening

It is fashionable at present for teeth to be whitened. There are different types of treatment but many may have side effects. If a young person wishes to have their teeth whitened they should research the different schemes thoroughly. Teeth whitening is not available on the National Health so the cost may be very high.

Young people with special needs

All the above apply though there may be additional considerations such as:
- Some young people with medical or learning difficulties may find dental treatment frightening. The treatment may also be difficult. Discuss this with the dentist as to how you may help.
- The dentist may recommend fluoride drops or tablets or the use of a toothpaste with a higher fluoride content.
- More frequent visits to the dentist may be necessary.
- To prevent decay, a plastic coating may be applied to the chewing surface of the back teeth.
- Toothbrushes can be adapted if necessary or other mouth cleaning aids may be provided.
- Whether the young person can properly wear, clean and care for a tooth brace.

A young person suffering dental pain, who is unable to express discomfort may exhibit a change in behaviour which may include the following – loss of appetite, unwillingness to participate in usual activities, disturbed sleep, irritability or self injury.

School leavers, particularly those with mild learning disabilities, may lose contact with dental services especially when these were provided in school. Similarly, adults with severe learning disabilities who do not attend day services may not receive appropriate oral care. This needs to be highlighted when planning for leaving care.

The British Dental Health Foundation website is worth a visit.

Drug and solvent abuse

WHAT TO DO IN AN EMERGENCY

- Make sure they've got fresh air.

- Turn them on their side so they won't choke on their vomit.

- Don't leave them alone.

- Get someone to dial 999 and ask for an ambulance.

- Collect any powders, tablets or anything else they may have been using and give it all to the paramedics when the ambulance arrives.

Drug abuse

Many young people will have experimented with drugs in some form before they leave school.

? *Why do they do it?*

- They may feel lonely and inadequate or lack self-esteem or confidence and think that taking drugs will help.
- They think it will help them 'blot out' problems.
- They are encouraged by their friends or made to look small if they refuse.
- They might have been tricked or bullied into taking them and become hooked.
- It's an alternative to using alcohol or solvents.
- They like the excitement, the element of danger.
- If adults are shocked, that can be an attraction.
- They like experimenting with new sensations.
- Hallucinations and sensations can be interesting and exciting but can also be dangerous, unpleasant and frightening.
- Drugs allow young people to escape – albeit temporarily and only in their imagination.

Signs and symptoms

There are often no clear-cut signs and many of the effects are hard to distinguish from normal growing up. Many teenagers are moody without having taken drugs. Look out for:

- Any sudden change in behaviour or lifestyle, for example, going around with a new set of friends.
- Wide swings in mood or behaviour – depression, lethargy, followed by being outgoing, active or chatty.
- Loss of appetite.
- Being unusually aggressive.
- Being unusually drowsy or sleepy.
- Asking for money from their friends or carers without explaining what it is for or with feeble explanations.
- Loss of money or other objects from the house.
- Secretiveness or lying.
- Unusual stains, marks or smells on the body or clothes or around the house.

Don't jump to conclusions, but be alert to signs such as:
- scorched pieces of tin foil
- a home-made pipe
- the remains of a cannabis cigarette with small cardboard tube filter
- dilated pupils in the eyes
- rash around the mouth

? *What drugs might they take?*

Unfortunately, there are many different drugs available to young people. They include:

- cannabis
- magic mushrooms
- hallucinogens
- amphetamines or speed
- barbiturates
- benzodiazephines

- ecstasy
- cocaine
- crack
- heroin
- solvents

These often have 'street' names which may change with fashion.

Most areas will have places such as youth advisory centres, GP surgeries and schools where you or the young person can get help with their problem if required. There are very good booklets published which give facts about the many drugs available including the other names that might be used, what they look like, how they are taken, the effects, the health risks and their legal status.

These booklets usually use the word 'parent' as an abbreviation for any adult responsible for a young person. They also note that the term 'drugs' refers to illegal drugs, but prescribed drugs taken inappropriately and household products can also be abused.

Injecting drugs

Many young people will try taking drugs and stop immediately. Sadly others will not. Injecting drugs can be the most dangerous because of the risks of:

- *Infection* where injecting equipment is unsterile and shared. The most serious infections are HIV (which can develop into AIDS) and hepatitis. If a young person is injecting drugs they may get hepatitis B. Make sure they know the immediate dangers – for example, using the wrong injection methods – and get help for the long term but in the short term make sure they get a supply of clean needles. (Sometimes these are available free from Drugs Advisory Centres).
- *Abscesses and thrombosis* and other conditions from injecting drugs that were never intended for injection.
- *Gangrene* from hitting an artery instead of a vein.
- *Blood poisoning* caused by a wound becoming infected.
- *Overdose* when a drug of unknown strength is delivered directly into the bloodstream.

The question of drug abuse should be discussed at the young person's planning meetings or reviews where any decisions will be made about how to manage it.

? *What to do if a young person is 'high'*

- Keep calm and be patient – you have got to try to bring them down.
- Talk to them about how they feel at that moment.
- Ask them questions about where they are or what they can see – they may be suffering from hallucinations. One young person said he saw 'pink elephants' but the changes may be more subtle for other young people. The effects will be different for each individual. Sometimes these hallucinations persist even after the person is 'sober' again.
- Gradually, slowly, quietly, explain where they are, who you are.
- Keep talking, don't threaten, be pleasant – the time for punishments (if appropriate) and explanations may be later.
- Sometimes just to leave them to themselves is the best solution but you will need to stay alert.

How to help prevent drug abuse:

- Talk to the young people about their views on drugs or their experience of drugs.
- Help them have new, interesting and challenging experiences as an alternative and diversion away from taking drugs.
- Get them to think about how they might refuse drugs without losing their friends.
- Teach them to care for and value their health.
- Help them build up their self-esteem and respect for themselves.
- Treat them with respect.
- Take an interest in their opinions and worries.
- Check out any problems they may have.

Solvent abuse

After smoking and alcohol, 'glue sniffing', as it is commonly called, is the most common form of teenage experimentation. Young people often start as young as 8-9 years but the peak age is 13-14 years.

They might sniff:

- butane gas (in cigarette lighters and refill canisters)
- aerosol sprays including deodorants
- correcting fluids
- solvent-based glues
- dry-cleaning fluids
- the contents of some types of fire extinguishers
- thinners
- petrol
- liquid shoe polish
- almost any other household product

The reasons why young people try glue sniffing are much the same as those that make them abuse any other drug (see page 46)

? *What should I look for?*

There are no clear-cut signs and many of the effects are hard to distinguish from normal growing up. Moodiness may be a result of sniffing but many teenagers are moody without having tried solvents.

Signs to watch out for include:
- Finding quantities of empty butane, aerosol or glue cans, or plastic bags in a place where you know young people have been.
- Chemical smell on clothes or breath.
- 'Drunken' behaviour.
- Any sudden change in behaviour or lifestyle, for example, going around with a new set of friends.
- Wide swings in mood or behaviour.
- Spots around nose and mouth – 'glue sniffers' rash' only occurs with some glues and may not be as common as acne!
- Loss of appetite.
- Asking for money from their friends or carers without explaining what it is for, or with feeble explanations.
- Secretiveness about leisure-time activities.
- Frequent and persistent headaches, sore throat or runny nose – a quick visit to the doctor would be wise.

Don't jump to conclusions, but be alert to the signs.

A young person told us:

> Solvent abuse is dangerous because the initial 'buzz' only lasts seconds so a continual use is needed to keep the high going, which can lead to suffocation.

How to help
Most young people who try sniffing will only do it a few times and stop without any help from adults. But if you find a young person has tried solvents it is important to deal with it calmly:
- They may not realise that it is dangerous so telling them of the dangers may be all they need.
- Don't nag or preach, talk to them, show you are concerned, help them to change their ways.
- Be a good listener – perhaps there are problems you don't know about. These problems may be far more important than the sniffing.
- If they have been sniffing for some time, arrange a health check.
- It may be difficult to stop a determined sniffer, so stay alert.
- Arrange other activities together – it will show you care and will give them other things to do. It will also help you to keep track of how they are using their free time.
- Suggest they join a youth club, take part in physical activities or trips out of town – it'll give them a chance to meet new groups of young people.
- For those young people who refuse to stop using solvents you may want to give advice on how to avoid, or reduce damage to their health.

Eating disorders

Some young people have a physical eating condition which they may have had since birth. You should be given all the relevant information if the young person still has a problem. Other young people, however, may develop an emotional eating disorder.

> My brother tries to be perfect in every way. He worries all the time about what other people think of him.

My friend sometimes starts eating and just can't stop.

My sister has become very distant from us. She seems to keep herself away from us.

Some of the above signs might mean that someone has an emotional eating disorder. People with an eating problem may eat too much, or refuse to eat, because they are unhappy. This can lead to emotional and physical problems. People often think that eating disorders are just about food and weight, but they are not. They are about feelings as well. People often don't think that young people might have this illness. Eating disorders are a way of coping with feelings that are causing unhappiness or depression. It may be difficult to face up to, and talk about, feelings like anger, sadness, guilt, loss or fear. The eating disorder is an unconscious attempt to avoid these feelings, or to keep them under control. It is a sign that the young person needs help in coping with life and shows how they see themselves as a person. There are many reasons why people develop eating disorders. Often there is no one cause, but a series of events that makes the young person unable to cope. Examples are:

- Changes in the family.
- The death of someone special.
- Problems at school e.g. exams or being bullied.
- Lack of confidence e.g. moving towards adolescence.
- Emotional or sexual abuse.

If carers think the young person has a particular problem with eating they should seek advice. It may be there is quite a simple reason that can easily be put right or the young person may need specialist help.

Two particular illnesses are:
1. *Anorexia nervosa*, with sufferers described as anorexic (not eating).
2. *Bulimia nervosa* with sufferers known as bulimic (eating too much and then making themselves sick, or taking laxatives to clear out the bowels).

Many specialists believe the two disorders are part of the same illness. In fact, bulimics have often been anorexics first. Nine out of ten people showing signs of eating disorders are women, the peak age being between 15 and 18 years.

Eating disorders are often an indication of a person's feelings about themselves. They are emotional disorders which focus on food and consumption. People who suffer may have:

- A drive to become thin.
- An obsession with food, weight, calories etc.
- A reliance on eating, or refusing to eat, in order to cope with emotional discomfort, stress or developmental changes.
- A view that the world values appearances over personality.

Research has shown that young people who suffer from eating disorders:

- May have been easy-going young people who did not answer back.
- Made less fuss and got less angry.
- Are often good students and high achievers.
- May be anxious to please and to live up to other people's expectations of them.
- Are often very secretive and try to hide their illness.

Stress, anxiety, loneliness and depression may trigger off the illness.

If you think there is a problem, the young person should contact their GP or the Eating Disorders Association – www.eatingdisorderscentre.co.uk They may need your help to do this.

Many people know that anorexia and bulimia are eating disorders, but people who are obese may have similar problems with food, and need just as much help and sympathy.

Eczema

Eczema affects the skin. The key to treatment is to keep the skin moist with regular emollients (greasy creams, bath oils, ointment) and treat flare up with steroids or antibiotics as directed by your GP.

Eye care

Lazy eye' and 'squint' are two very important conditions. A young child can become blind in a 'lazy' or 'squinting' eye if it is not treated. Treatment varies, but may include eye exercises, patching the good eye to make the lazy one work, a simple operation or wearing glasses. Some children who have eye problems will not have been treated when they are young. Urgent help should be sought so the condition can be improved if at all possible. Young people's eyes should be checked regularly. They should go to the optician once a year as a minimum. Young people should also be encouraged to wear any glasses prescribed.

> **Regular eye tests are essential.**

Foot care

Many people hate trainers and think they are bad for a young person's feet, particularly if they are made from synthetic materials. This may be true but a well-fitting trainer is better than an ill-fitting shoe. What is important is that:
- The young person's socks fit well.
- The young person's feet are measured regularly until their feet stop growing.
- The correct size shoes are worn.
- The shoes support the feet properly.

Persuading teenagers to follow the above guidelines will not be an easy task!

Growing up, facts of life, puberty and sexual health

Some young people may be upset if their physical or sexual development is slower than that of their friends. Disabled young people may also be equally sensitive if their sexual development is delayed or disordered.

Young people can be extremely sensitive even if outwardly they may appear morose or cocky. There will be media pressure and peer group pressure for young adolescents to behave in a particular way. One day they may act very responsibly and well, the next they will revert to being very childish or rude. The young person probably won't know why they react or feel or behave the way they do.

Young people at this time particularly need a warm caring environment, consistent handling, constant re-assurance, someone they can talk to about their worries and someone who is patient and who understands and respects the young person's privacy. The most valuable thing you can give a young person is your time; time to listen, time to talk and time to understand.

Young people who are looked after may have changed schools or been off school for sometime so may well have missed out on sex education lessons. It may also be that because of their family circumstances they will not have been told about such matters at home.

Looked after children are also more likely to have poor sexual health, be at risk of sexual exploitation and experience early parenthood. Your employer should give you guidance for foster carers on sex and relationship education. Within this section there is a discussion on sexual matters including gay, lesbian and transgender (LBGT) issues.

It is therefore essential that carers give help and guidance, otherwise a young person's only knowledge may have been gained from the playground or through their negative earlier experiences. In addition to explaining the biological facts, the carer could consider discussions around:

- morals
- caring
- the law
- ethics
- relationships
- genuine affection
- love
- responsibility
- culture
- sexuality
- respect

Some young people may need extra help to understand about the meaning of relationships. Young people who have been sexually abused will need particular help to understand that what happened to them was wrong and have confidence that they can have healthy and sustaining relationships. In fact a young person may disclose that they have been sexually abused during such a discussion. Carers should always ask for professional help if this occurs.

Different words may also have different meanings in different families. It will help if carers can find out what a young person knows or what words were used by their family or previous carer.

Young people need to know about life cycles, reproduction and puberty and to understand about the changes that take place to their bodies. They also need to know about the gradual lead-up to these changes.

If the young person does ask questions, the carer needs to be prepared, and to be honest, frank and truthful in their answers. There are many very good leaflets available which also answer many of the questions a young person may ask. The carer may have to tell the young person several times about the facts of life etc. as the young person may forget or may not fully understand the first time.

If the young person missed the sex education lessons at school and the carer is going to explain things to the young person, then the carer should tell the school so the teachers understand if the young person starts asking questions about sex.

Always advise parents when the young person is receiving sex education. If possible, invite parents to be present at any discussion or explanation that takes place. This will help parents to recognise a young person's new needs.

Finding the right opportunity to talk to the young person is very important. If the young person starts asking questions relating to sex or reproduction this is obviously a natural way to begin. If a young person starts making sexual innuendoes or masturbating then this could also lead into a discussion on sex. Whenever you decide the time is right, privacy and confidentiality are essential. Using the right words is also important. Some young people get very embarrassed if very explicit words or pictures are used.

A young person may be very naive or very knowledgeable – or think they are very knowledgeable. Whatever the case, the carer needs to be well prepared beforehand. They should also be willing to say *'I don't know but let's find out'* if necessary. A head teacher told me that despite an apparent broadening of attitudes, boys still giggle and seem to find sex lessons more difficult to handle than girls of a similar age.

There is likely to be much misunderstanding about the whole question of sex and puberty. What is important is that the young person feels able to talk to you and to discuss such matters openly, frankly and without embarrassment.

Support and advice should be available from your school nurse or designated LAC nurse. They will be able to access leaflets, books and videos, to help you in this vital area of work. Your local authority may have a policy on sex and sex education, and may also offer training. Do speak to your SSW about what might be available.

Disabled young people may need more help and support. They will have the same urges and many of the developmental changes as others but may find expressing it difficult.

Different families and cultures will have their own morals and rules about sex. For some, sex and the workings of the body are very private and discussion is taboo. Sometimes young people who have been told 'It's wrong to touch, kiss or to talk about sex' become confused. Other families and cultures will prefer a more open approach seeing sex as part of normal life. However, when openness becomes permissiveness, problems occur.

There are many myths and different beliefs surrounding puberty both from a cultural and religious point of view. Local health promotion clinics or sexual health clinics should be able to provide information and advice.

Periods

Many young girls will start their periods at 10 or 11 years of age, others may start earlier or much later. Whenever it is, they need to be prepared, both physically and mentally. They need to know about:

- Sanitary towels and tampons – they should always have a packet stored in their bedroom and also some in their school bag so they are ready for the start of their periods.
- Period pains.
- Vaginal discharge that starts sometime before their periods begin.
- The many bodily changes that will be occurring at that time.

Help them to look forward to this new phase in their life.

Informed decisions on sexual health issues

Below are some specific guidelines drawn up after a challenge was made in the courts as to whether a young person could make their own decisions regarding sexual health matters without having to refer back to their parent or guardian. These guidelines are usually referred to by health and social care professionals as the Fraser Guidelines (they are an updated version of the previously used Gillick Guidelines).

The Fraser Guidelines outline how and whether a young person you are caring for is able to make their own informed decisions. They state that a young person can give informed consent for sexual advice if:

- The young person understands the health professional's advice.
- The health professional cannot persuade the young person to inform their parent or allow the doctor to inform the parents that they are seeking contraceptive advice.
- The young person is very likely to begin, or continue having, intercourse with or without contraception.
- Unless they receive contraceptive advice or treatment, the young person's physical or mental health are likely to suffer.
- The young person's best interests require the health professional to give contraceptive advice or treatment without parental consent.

Contraception

There are many different types of contraception. Advice on the best methods for individuals and on how to use the particular form of contraception is available from family planning clinics, GP surgeries, sexual health clinics and youth advisory centres. There are also many leaflets which the carer might keep at home in case the young person asks questions. However, what is important is that young people are able to discuss contraception with their carer which includes discussing relationships and responsibilities.

The male condom is the only form of contraception that a man uses, all the other forms listed below are used by women.

Male and female condoms: These are some of the most effective forms of contraception and there are no side effects. A male condom is said to be as high as 98% effective and the female condom is about 95% effective in preventing unwanted pregnancies if used properly. They are also the most effective method to use in the prevention of sexually transmitted diseases (STIs).

The male condom is the most commonly used of this method.

How to use the male condom:

- Hold the tip of the condom to remove the air while the condom is rolled all the way. The tip will need to stick out as this is where the sperm will gather.
- If it is not rolling down easily it may be on inside out – you will need to use a new condom and start again.
- As soon as the man has ejaculated (come) ensure you hold the condom firmly and slowly pull off the condom to ensure you do not spill any of the sperm.

Tips on using the male condom

- Ensure that it is still within the sell-by date on the packet and that the packet has not been interfered with (this also applies to the female condom).
- Take care that the condom is not pierced by sharp fingernails or jewellery as this can make it split and therefore be ineffective.
- Make sure the condom does not come into contact with any oil-based products, for example body oil, as this will weaken the condom causing it to split or tear.

The combined pill: If taken according to instructions this method is reported to be 99% effective. The combined pill also is credited with reducing period pains and pre-menstrual symptom and has been shown to protect against ovarian cancer.

The pills come in monthly supplies with dates to help ensure that one is taken for each of the relevant 21 days. Young women will then not take anything for a period of seven days (during which time they will have their period) and will then start taking the pills again.

One of the drawbacks is that they do need to be taken regularly and at the same time of the day otherwise they may not be effective and there may be a risk of getting pregnant.

Progestogen-only pill: Some women will not be able to take the combined pill as they may suffer unwanted side effects. The progestogen pill is an alternative and is taken in the same way.

Contraceptive patch: These are used for a week at a time for three weeks and then, like the pill, there will be a patch free week to enable the young woman to have her period. This method is said to be 99% effective if taken according to the instructions given.

The diaphragm or cap: The effectiveness for this method is between 92-95% and depends not only on it being used correctly but also on the type of diaphragm used as there is a variety of types available. As with other methods, young people and foster carers can get advice on these matters to enable the young person to make better choices that would fit into their lifestyle. Using a diaphragm would mean young people would need to be prepared and diligent if they are to prevent unwanted pregnancies. As with condoms, the diaphragm is made from the same material and so cannot be used with any oil-based products as they could damage the diaphragm and therefore affect its ability to protect.

The contraceptive injection: This method is considered extremely effective. There are two types – one gives protection for eight weeks and the other for 12 weeks.

Implants (IUS or IUD): Implants are considered very effective and have the longest period of protection ranging from 3-10 years. As with other forms of contraception, young people will need to have full information before considering implants.

> **Please note: only the condom will offer protection against
> sexually transmitted infections!**

Sexually transmitted infections (STIs)

Unless you are fully protected you will risk catching an STI. It can happen the first time you have sex, the sex does not have to have been fully penetrative and they can also be transmitted through same sex relationships.

There are more than 25 known STIs but the most common are:
- Chlamydia
- Herpes
- Genital wart
- Gonorrhoea
- NSU (Non-specific urethritis)

Less common but still widespread are:
- Hepatitis B
- TV (Trichomonas vaginalis)
- Public lice (crabs)
- Scabies
- Syphilis
- HIV (can lead to AIDS)

Symptoms: Sometimes, especially for women there may not be clear symptom but below are the most noticeable:
- smelly discharge from the penis or the vagina
- burning or pain when peeing
- itches, rashes, lumps, ulcers, sores or blisters around the genital area
- pain – in the genitals, during sex, in the testicles or lower abdomen
- for women there may be bleeding, between periods, after sex

Treatment: Most STIs can be completely cured if they are diagnosed early so it is very important that you do not delay seeking advice and treatment should you suspect you have been exposed to an STI. The symptoms in women are often more difficult to determine so it is necessary for there to be openness and honesty between sexual partners. It is also absolutely necessary not to have sex until the condition has completely cleared.

Tests and the treatment can be carried out by:
- Sexual Health Clinics (usually located in hospitals)
- Genitourinary Medicine (GUM) Clinics or
- Sexually Transmitted Infection (STI) Clinics

Some tests will be diagnosed while you wait but other tests will take longer and it is necessary not to have sex during this time.

Treatment would usually be in the form of:
- antibiotics (it is important to take the full dosage prescribed)
- lotions (for crabs and scabies)

There is no complete cure for HIV but there are many options developed which can enable people to live comfortably.

There are some very good charities where young people and foster carers can obtain both confidential as well as practical advice and help on contraception, sex and relationships, sexual development, pregnancy and STIs. Below are two specific ones:
- fpa
- Brook

Both have websites and there are other useful sites such as www.teenagehealthfreak.co.uk.

Hay fever

This causes sneezing and running eyes and nose. Young people allergic to tree pollens (e.g. silver birch) tend to wheeze in spring. Those allergic to grass are affected in the summer. Many of these conditions may appear worse in times of stress.

Health assessments

If a young person is asked to have a health assessment they have the right to refuse, providing they are of a sufficient age to understand what is going on. However, statutory health needs assessments should be encouraged by the carer and promoted to the young person as an opportunity to air any of their health worries or needs in confidence. If the young person does refuse then the carer must inform their local health services. They can then discuss any concerns they may have and the health team will offer support and advice to the carer and the young person as appropriate.

A young person who has been abused may be very worried about having a medical examination and will need re-assurance and help to overcome these fears. Health assessments should be done as soon as the young person enters care and offered annually for older teenagers up until the age of 16 when they may wish to deal with their health as and when they need to by attending their GP practice when they are ill.

Every effort should be made to address the health issues that are identified in the health assessment, and any difficulties should be reported to the school nurse or the designated nurse for looked after young people (either the local one or the one from the area that the young person came from).

Health records

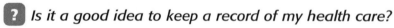 *Is it a good idea to keep a record of my health care?*

Yes, because:
- Later in life we are often asked to fill in forms about our medical records and it helps to remember detail.
- Young people can take their records with them if they move somewhere else.
- They may find there is a pattern of regular illness. By looking at their records and thinking what they have done they may be able to work out why.

Carers will have guidelines as to what is required whilst a young person is in care:
- Young people should be offered a health assessment every year and be involved in the formulation of their health care plan following an assessment.

- Their eyes should be tested as necessary.
- Dental check ups are recommended every six months.

Encourage them to continue this when they become independent. There is a health record sheet on pages 61 and 62 that young people might like to use when they are no longer in care.

Carers must also keep a record of any medicines the young people have taken or must take.

Hearing

Young people who have not had their hearing problems resolved when they are young are likely to have listening or attention difficulties which may persist into later life. Poor hearing makes it difficult for a young person to understand the teacher in class which may lead to behaviour or learning difficulties. Other young people may also ignore them. The hearing of young people suffering from glue ear is intermittently affected so repeated testing is necessary. You may be able to spot a hearing problem if the young person:

- Turns up the volume on the television.
- Shouts rather than speaks.
- Doesn't come when called (if not facing you).
- Doesn't form words correctly.
- Behaves very boisterously or disruptively.
- Gets into trouble and does not achieve at school.

Research has shown that having earphones in the ear playing loud music for more than an hour a day will cause hearing loss which cannot be put right later. Loud music can also affect hearing. It is essential that young people do not listen to music for long periods especially at high volume.

HIV and AIDS

- **HIV** is a virus that can get into the blood and destroy the white blood cells leaving the body open to attack from other infections.
- **AIDS** is a condition which develops when the body's defences are not working properly. This means people are more likely to get illnesses which the body would normally be able to fight off easily.

These illnesses can be serious or fatal since, at the moment, there is no complete cure for AIDS.

? *How is the HIV virus passed on?*

- Through intimate unprotected sexual contact or intercourse between a man and a woman, between men or between women.
- Needles or syringes which have been used by an infected person. Drug misusers are especially at risk.
- Occasionally women who have the virus can pass it on to their babies during pregnancy, at birth or through breast milk.

You cannot catch the virus by touching objects used by an infected person or by touching an infected person. All donated blood is tested before it is used in hospitals and blood products are heat-treated to reduce the risk of infection.

Young people will have heard a lot about HIV and AIDS and will often be scared because of what they have heard. Talk to them openly about sex and about drug taking and substance abuse covered within this section. If they follow the simple guidelines they will reduce the risk of catching AIDS. If a young person is HIV positive or has AIDS they will need extra help and support as well as education on just what it all means and how it will affect them. Ask your social worker for advice or guidance if a young person is HIV positive.

Mental health, emotional health and well-being

Some people say they are depressed when they really don't mean it. Young people may think they are:

- sad
- miserable
- mad

- unhappy
- bad
- really upset

In most cases their state of mind will soon change but if you feel the unhappiness is sustained then you should seek professional help.

There are a number of issues that concern people who work with young people in care – all of which relate to their emotional health and well being. If you were to ask people to list what comes to mind when thinking about the term 'mental health', you will usually get a list of mental illnesses – illustrating the fact that, in this country, 'mental health' is interpreted as 'mental illness'. Sadly society seems to dictate that mental illness is something to hide and to be ashamed of which prevents young people and their carers seeking appropriate help until small problems become crises. For young people who are in care or who have spent time in care they are particularly vulnerable as the disruptions in their lives impact very heavily on their choices for the future.

- How do they know where they belong?
- Have they had many other life changes?
- How do they know who they are?
- How do they learn and discover when they find themselves in a continual state of angst, always fearful that their life will dramatically change?

Living in a secure and safe environment, having plenty of good food, exercise and support can go a long way to helping a young person overcome some of their anxieties and worries. Young people who have emotional health problems should have access to timely, integrated, high quality, multi-disciplinary health services to ensure effective assessment, treatment and support, for them and their families.

In other words, get help sooner rather than later. If you are not satisfied with the service, then keep going until the young person receives the help and support to which they are entitled.

There are mental health issues that are usually highlighted at school as it affects the young person's educational development. Details of the following and how to help the young person are included in the Education chapter:

- Dyslexia
- Attachment disorder
- ADHD/ADD
- Autistic Spectrum Disorder (Autism)
- Dyspraxia
- Foetal Alcohol Syndrome disorder

Personal hygiene

Make sure young people know about the need to wash thoroughly and use a deodorant at least once a day. They should also wash their hands after using the toilet. Changing into clean clothes regularly is essential. Young people also need to be told of the consequences if they don't! With the changes that take place in both boys and girls during puberty it is particularly important that personal hygiene is stressed as they are likely to sweat more and it can be very smelly.

Preventative medicine

Preventative medicine empowers everyone to take control of their lives. It can range from self-examination of breasts and testicles to awareness of the possible side effects of prescribed drugs.

The diet and lifestyle of young people can have a significant affect on their health in later life. Other areas that are important are:

- Trying to reduce accidents amongst young people, especially those accidents which occur in the home.
- Persuading the rider *and the passenger* to wear protective clothing on motor bikes including properly fitting helmets.
- Encouraging young people to take cycling proficiency tests and to wear cycle helmets.
- Reminding them that accidents are common whilst under the influence of drugs or alcohol.
- Encouraging them to give up smoking.

Smoking

> Smoking kills   Smoking causes cancer

These are just two statements that must now be printed on cigarette packets as a warning. The biggest single thing in anyone's life they can do to prevent heart disease is to not smoke, or to give up smoking.

There is a lot of pressure for young people to smoke – from their peers, from films and from older people they admire. It is illegal for young people under 16 to buy cigarettes or tobacco. Education about the dangers of smoking is a must for everyone. Too often smoking is seen as a normal part of growing up without anyone realising the harm it causes. It is addictive, so giving up will not be easy. It is also expensive.

Don't preach, just encourage quitting – the decision must be their own. You could agree a programme to give up smoking with them and help them stick to it. You cannot make anyone give up smoking if they don't want to, but here are some tips which may help:
- Don't nag or lecture.
- Help them to get through day-by-day.
- Encourage them to get more help from a website or local clinic.
- Encourage them to go to a smoking cessation clinic. Most GPs will be able to direct you to the nearest one.
- Keep them occupied.
- Provide sugar free gum whenever they want a cigarette.
- Avoid places where people are smoking.
- Plan a reward with the money saved.
- Remember that a slip up with one or two cigarettes does not put people back to square one, just resolve that the next day will be even better.

No young person under the age of 16 should be prescribed nicotine patches. Some young people actually do not smoke 'properly', and therefore are not truly at risk or addicted, and the use of patches could be dangerous. Nicotine patches are also highly addictive and could lead to a true addiction for the young person concerned. If you would like further help and guidance in encouraging your young person to give up smoking, contact your school nurse, call in at your local clinic or try www.quit.org.uk and www.nosmokingday.org.uk

Passive smoking is breathing other people's cigarette smoke. Not only can it cause irritation to eyes, nose and throat, headaches, dizziness and sickness, it can cause asthma and allergies to worsen and increase the risk of cancer by up to 30%.

In reality many young people in care are smokers. They are often physically and emotionally dependent on cigarettes so it may be necessary to work with them to set permissible boundaries that are acceptable to smokers and non-smokers alike. House rules on smoking must be kept by everyone. Ensure no one smokes in the house or in the car.

Sun

Too many young people think having a suntan not only makes them feel good but they think it gives them sex appeal too! It has been proved that spending too much time in the sun is not a good idea and can cause skin cancer. Here are a few tips:
- Above all, *don't burn*, tan slowly – gradually increasing the time spent in the sun each day.
- Always use the appropriate sunscreens for different types of skin.
- Avoid the midday sun.
- Wear a sun hat.
- Wear a good pair of sunglasses.
- Everyone's skin can burn but people with fair skin, usually those with blond or red hair, are particularly vulnerable.

Health record sheet 1

Name _____ Blood Group _____

Name and address of doctor _____

_____

_____

Telephone number _____

Date	Treatment

Date	Type of Injection

✎ Health record sheet 2

Name

Name and address of DENTIST

Telephone number

Date	Treatment

Name and address of OPTICIAN

Telephone number

Date	Treatment/Advice

Section 6
Education

Education is the key to a successful future.

Parental (carer) involvement in a young person's schooling for a young person between the ages of 7 and 16 is a more powerful force than family background, size of family and level of parental education.

Charles Desforges, 2003

Problems and solutions

Education is a good way to build a sound future. Lots of research about young people has shown how worried they are about their education. Young people really need your help to get the best from education. There is a very helpful document entitled 'Who does what. How social workers and carers can support the education of looked after children?' If you want to know more or would like a copy of the booklet go to the dfes website.

Possible problems:
- Young people get worried that they are getting behind with their work because of poor attendance; this often makes them not want to go to school which makes matters worse.
- Perhaps their concentration has not been as good as it should be – worries, disturbances or neglect may well be the cause.
- They have had frequent changes of schools.
- The time taken to get them into a school after a move was too long.
- They have not been getting enough extra help to enable them to catch up.
- Home tutoring or attendance at a pupil referral unit has not been available soon or often enough if there was a problem with school.
- There has been no place that was quiet where they could do their homework.
- They may have been treated differently at school by other young people and occasionally by staff.
- If they are disabled they might have problems moving about the building or about the way they are taught.
- They may have been teased.
- They may lack confidence to ask the teacher if they don't understand.
- They don't have any friends at the school so misbehave or 'show off' to draw attention to themselves.
- They need help to build up their self esteem and confidence.

Here are some solutions other carers have suggested:
- Contact the education office to get things speeded up, in order to get a young person back into school or being home tutored or anything else that may be needed.
- Help them discretely with their weaker subjects.
- If you don't feel you can help them with their homework find someone else who can help them.
- There should be a named person in each school and a specific person in each local authority who has responsibility for the young person's education. Contact them and ask for their advice or help.

- If the young person is disabled make sure the school has suitable access facilities – there is a law regarding access and equality of opportunity.
- Make sure there is a place set aside especially for homework.
- Attend open evenings, school events and sports days.
- Work with all concerned to ensure they have a personal education plan (PEP) and that it is up to date and relevant and help the young person to achieve the targets.
- If there seems to be a problem contact, sooner rather than later, the designated teacher, head teacher, educational social worker (may be known by another name in different local authorities) or any other person you think might be able to help.
- There should be a computer available for all children and young people in care for their personal use. Ensure the young person has this and speak to their social worker if they do not have one.
- There are out of school learning opportunities. These provide learning experience outside school hours for pupils and families. Extended schools are where the different agencies work together to help children and young people to achieve their potential in all aspects of their life including learning.
- Many schools have learning mentors to help young people make the most of their school life. A learning mentor is:
  - a role model
  - an active listener
  - an observer
  - an encourager
  - a challenger of assumptions
  - a guide
  - a target negotiator
  - a reliable, approachable, non-judgemental and realistic support with pupils, parents, carers and staff

Mentors may be asked to help with:
- A young person who is finding it difficult to settle in a new school.
- A young person who is getting behind with coursework or homework.
- A young person from a different culture or background to others around them.
- A young person who is facing a particular challenge at home, e.g. separation, coming into care or a bereavement.
- A young person who is having difficulty with friendships.
- A young person who finds it difficult to speak out in class.

Carers should:
- Have high expectations but be aware of the young person's limitation to ensure they achieve and do not get disheartened.
- Encourage them, praise them, and show an interest in all they do.
- Show they care.

Other ways to help

Some young people will find that the education system does not meet their needs. Work based alternatives may be the answer. There is an education/employer taskforce whose aim is to help young people gain skills in the work place. Another option may be for them to attend a local college that offers a specific course for pre-16 young people.

The question of feeling that they are being treated differently because of where they are living such as in a children's home is not a new one. It may be due to a lack of understanding, but if it is upsetting the young person then you may need to go to the school to try to sort out the problem.

Many examinations include a good deal of coursework so if a young person changes school at 14, 15 or 16 they may not be able to take all their exams as their coursework may have become lost or there is a different examination syllabus' at the new school. It is especially important that 'all the stops are pulled out' to try to get the young person to stay at their existing school if possible.

For young people not to be educated to their full potential is not acceptable. If you, or the young person's social worker, do not seem to be getting their education sorted, you could try contacting: the person responsible for liaison with education, the education office, your local councillor, in fact anyone you think might help.

Extended schools may be helpful both for the young person and for the carer. They may offer:
- High quality 'wraparound' service provided on the school site or through other local providers, available 8am-6pm all year round.
- A variety of activities such as homework clubs and study support, sport, music tuition, special interest clubs and volunteering.
- Parent and carer support including information sessions for them at key transition points, parenting programmes and family learning sessions.
- Swift and easy referral to a wide range of specialist support services such as speech and language therapy, family support services and behaviour support.
- Wider community access to ICT (information computer technology), sports and arts facilities, including adult learning.

Encourage the young people to take part in as many different activities both in school and in the community to widen their horizons and to help develop their self-esteem. Encourage them to go on school trips if at all possible.

Sometimes a young person will need to understand a different language at school from that which is spoken at home. Carers need to help the young person accordingly, and a specialist teacher or advisor may need to be provided.

Carers should give the school the names of people who are not allowed to see or meet the young person. The school will also be involved, and be a part of the protection plan, for a young person who has been the subject of child protection proceedings or where there may be continuing risks to the young person. It is very important to work closely with the school.

It is also important that the young person gets to school punctually.

When they come home each day from school:
- Have a warm welcoming environment for them.
- Offer them a drink and talk about what has happened to them during the day. They may not want to talk about school straight away.
- Tell them what you've been doing during the day too.
- Encourage them to change out of their school clothes.

If a young person tells you about their worries, ask them what they would like you to do.

Don't put pressure on a young person to achieve your goals...but have high expectations. They will never know what is achievable until they try.

Partnership with parents and carers

Success in the education of all young people depends, at least in some part, on the involvement of their parents and carers. If a young person sees that they are enthusiastic about education, they are far more likely to view their schooling in a positive light, and be more receptive to learning. Some examples are:

- *Better home-school communication* for example, on issues such as pupil progress, information on what pupils will be taught, homework, and domestic concerns that may affect the pupils' ability to learn effectively.
- *Parents, carers and teachers working together on issues of concern* for example, aspirations, expectations, behaviour, bullying and drug education.
- *Parents and carers supporting and helping the young person's learning at home more effectively.*
- *The identification of issues that need to be addressed* within the school.

Young people out of school

If the young person is out of school for any reason:

- The carer must inform the school.
- The school should provide school work for the young person to do.
- The carer should ensure this work is done and returned to the school for marking and further work received.
- If the young person is suspended then a structured school day should be organised at home. A young person should not see it as a chance to do nothing! They should not be allowed to just watch TV or go out unsupervised.

Carers should ensure that a young person is out of school as little as possible. This may mean suggesting that planning meetings, reviews or other appointments take place after school or at weekends. It may also mean that the carer has to personally take the young person into the school building to ensure that they actually arrive.

Education and school

Every young person who is in care should be allocated a designated teacher in their school or college who has overall responsibility for their education. Each young person should also have a *personal education plan* (PEP page 78). This document should be drawn up with the parents, carers, social workers and the designated teacher and any other person who may know something about the young person such as an educational psychologist and the young person. The school keeps and up-dates the PEP until the young person moves to another school or college. It is then forwarded to that school or college so that they know what help and guidance the particular young person needs. The PEP should be reviewed regularly and is normally considered at review meetings.

Schools aim to improve standards in all areas of school life and are also being supported to help young people with their social, emotional and behavioural skills.

❓ *What should carers find out before a young person starts at a school?*

This should be provided by the school:

- The school routines and rules.
- What school clothing is required (including PE and sports kit).
- The curriculum offered and the way the school is organised.
- Activities outside normal school hours.
- Details of other agencies who might be involved in the young person's welfare, such as speech therapists, health visitors, social services, educational welfare officers and educational psychologists.
- Details of the school governors.
- The procedures for informing the school about illness, holidays, and other absences and, if the young person is disabled, for collecting them at the end of the school day.
- The calendar for the school year.

Carers should:

- Support the young person in every way, not just when there is a problem.
- Ensure the young person gets any additional help they need, especially if they have changed schools several times.
- See the teacher regularly but remember that the teacher's time is precious. If you make an appointment, keep to it or telephone to say that you can't.
- Go to open evenings with parents if possible.
- Show an interest in their homework and help if asked, but the young person must learn to become responsible for doing it themselves, though some may need support throughout their educational life.
- Have a quiet place available where the young person can work.
- Fill in reply slips and return them straight away.
- Show an interest; talk and discuss; make plans; cultivate good working habits.
- Talk about the young person's education with the parents if appropriate.

Schools need to understand and assess the physical and learning difficulties of a young person so they can adjust their teaching methods and systems accordingly.

Carers should **not**:

- Compare the young person unfavourably with others of the same age.
- Encourage fighting back aggressively if another young person attacks. If possible, it's better to avoid or ignore the other young person.
- Allow late nights beyond normal bed times except for special occasions or at weekends.
- Tell their troubles to the young person. Young people don't understand, and can't help. It makes them distressed and insecure: and then you'll have another problem such as a young person not wanting to leave the carer to go to school.
- Be disappointed, irritated or show anxiety if the young person is slow to learn. That will make it even harder for them.

Always help the young person to succeed. Nothing succeeds like success.

Discipline

All schools should have a written policy setting out the standards of behaviour it expects. The policy should outline what the school will do if the young person's behaviour falls below these standards.

Young people should be made aware of the behaviour policy as well as the sanctions which schools have a legal right to impose if a pupil misbehaves. Sanctions might include:
- a reprimand
- a letter to parents or carers
- removal from a class or group
- loss of privileges
- confiscating something belonging to the young person if it is inappropriate for school e.g. mobile phone or music player
- detention

Truancy and exclusions

A young person who gets into serious trouble at school can be excluded for a fixed period of time. The school should contact the parent or carer by telephone on the day with a follow-up letter sent confirming the situation. A school will only permanently exclude a young person as a last resort when all else has failed.

Uninspiring lessons, learning difficulties, apathy, bullying, problems, both present and previously, in their home life and attachment issues may all be causes of why young people truant or why they behave in such a way that they are excluded from school. Learning mentors, counselling, parents' and carers' groups, breakfast clubs, home visits are some successful ways of helping these young people. Alternative education schemes such as trying to re-engage young people through projects and different ways of teaching numeracy, literacy and IT and college based courses which are often vocational can all be helpful. Finding ways to help young people to learn to express themselves and also to encourage them to take up new interests may also work for some young people.

Carers should ask the school Special Educational Needs Co-ordinator (SENCO page 78) or designated teacher which schemes are available in their area to help.

Education: a young person's checklist

Moving to another home doesn't necessarily mean you have to change schools, but sometimes you will have to choose another school for them. Most people change schools around their 11th birthday anyway.

? *If I have to change schools how do I choose a new one?*
There may not be much choice, depending on where you live, but if you have to choose a new school, your carer can go with you to look round the schools. Talk to the teachers and pupils and then decide, providing there is a vacancy.

? *What will it be like starting a new school?*

Some things may be done differently. Just remember:
- That everyone takes time to settle in somewhere new.
- To ask if you're not sure about anything.
- To talk any problems over with your carer or your friends.

? *How do I choose which subjects to study?*

When a young person is 13 or 14 they will have to decide which subjects they want to study until they are 16. You will be given talks on the subjects you can do and will probably have handouts to read.

Think about:
- How interesting do you find the subjects?
- Will they help you get the job or college course you want?
- Will there be a lot of reading to do?
- Will there be a lot of practical things to do?

You won't have a completely free choice because:
- The law says you have to learn certain subjects such as maths and English.
- Some subjects may clash on the school timetable.

? *What can I do when I'm 16?*

At 16, young people can:
- Go on to get more qualifications.
- Start a skills course at college such as bricklaying, gardening or word processing.
- Start on a training scheme.
- Start on an apprenticeship scheme.
- Improve their maths and English.

? *Why should I study further or do more training?*

- Many jobs need trained workers.
- Pay and prospects are likely to be better after further study.
- You will have a wider choice of jobs or careers.

? *What qualifications will I need?*

For some courses you will need to get certain grades in your examinations. For others you will only have to show you want to work hard.

? *What if I fail some of my exams?*

You can re-take most exams you fail – many people spend an extra year doing this – but it might be better for you to do a vocational (job-related) course instead. Your school or college will help you decide.

? *How long do courses last?*

Most courses last one or two years. Young people can apply to any college or school they wish but help with transport expenses will only be given in certain cases. Visit several different places where you could go with your carer, and find the one that suits you best.

? *What will it be like?*

There will be a lot of work to do and much of it will have to be done in your own time. You will also have to learn to attend on time and regularly without constant reminders. It will be hard work and you should expect this, but you will also find you are treated more like an adult than when you were at school. At college there will be all sorts of different people of all ages over 16. It will take a lot of getting used to.

Helping with homework

Carers might:
- Suggest the young person does homework as soon as it is received as the information will be fresh in their mind.
- Encourage them to speak up when they have a difficulty – you may be able to help or may be able to guide them.
- Ensure they have a good work/life balance.
- Find out about educational programmes on radio or television or educational information on the web.
- Find out about study support or homework clubs in your area.

Tackling coursework

Good coursework marks can boost exam grades. Carers can help by:
- Finding out about the curriculum and how much work needs to be done.
- Finding out when coursework is due and helping the young person make a schedule to complete it.
- Make sure they are clear about what is required and how many marks will be available.
- Find internet sites and safe chat rooms that can help with studying.
- Encourage them to print and save their work regularly if working on a computer and to save the material on a memory stick as well as the computer.
- Encourage them to talk to their teacher about any problems as early as possible.
- Ensure they have the right books and resources.

Aiding revision

Carers can help ease the pressure of exams by:
- Helping the young person to develop a revision timetable and helping them stick to it.
- Listening to them and find ways to support them.
- Encouraging them with praise and sometimes rewards.

Qualifications

Choices, choices, choices. It does seem that the more qualifications you have, the more choices you will have in getting a job, choosing a job you like, moving to another job and getting promotion. There are so many qualifications available at present that many people are not sure what they mean and how the levels compare with one another. A careers adviser should be able to give you details of the different qualifications and what they mean. You can also look on the web to get the most up-to-date information.

Education of young people with special educational needs

There are many Acts that cover the education of young people with special needs. There are often local support groups that carers and parents of young people with special needs may join which will provide support as well as provide useful information.

What are the main categories covered by legislation?
1. Young people who find learning significantly more difficult than the majority of young people of their age.
2. Young people with a disability (emotional or physical) that makes it hard for them to make use of ordinary schooling in the local area.

The Local Education Authority (LEA) also has a duty to ensure that young people with less significant difficulties also have their needs met. It is the governing body of schools that are responsible for ensuring that these needs are identified and met. When offering help to a young person, schools would normally do the following:
1. Identify the problem.
2. Agree the action, activities and resources needed.
3. Decide on parent or carer support.
4. Set targets and timescales.
5. Monitor and review.

Schools must publish information about policies and state the roles of governors, heads, special educational needs coordinators, designated teachers and other teachers.

The following are some of the particular learning difficulties a young person might experience. However, many conditions overlap. These difficulties are quite likely to be hereditary.

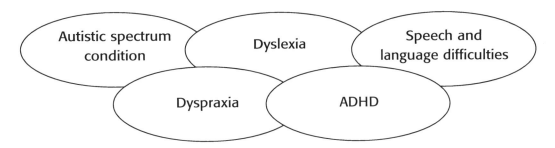

Diagram showing how many of the difficulties young people experience may be inter-linked

Up to 10 per cent of the whole population may have some degree of specific learning difficulty. In most cases this is likely to be fairly mild and can be managed within the classroom. In some cases additional help will be needed from the SENCO. Young people with specific learning difficulties, such as those above, should be entitled to additional time during tests and examinations. It is important that everyone knows this and that it is provided for the young person.

Dyslexia

Dyslexia is a difficulty with words, but it can involve more than just reading and spelling and can affect writing and number work. Dyslexia is often referred to as a specific learning difficulty to show that it is not an all-round learning problem, but is of a particular nature. This could be:

- An organising difficulty – for example, a child putting clothes on in the wrong order or back to front or a secondary school pupil not remembering which books are needed for which lesson.
- A word finding difficulty – for example, being unable to supply a word which is known and understood.
- A memory difficulty – which could be a poor short-term memory, a poor auditory memory (remembering things they hear), or sometimes a poor visual memory (remembering things they look at).
- A difficulty noticing how spoken words are broken up into syllables and individual sounds, and in hearing rhyme.
- Being poorly co-ordinated, which could make the young person appear clumsy.

Early diagnosis is very important. Most children will be diagnosed by the age of 7. However, some children in care 'slip through the net' so it is important they get an assessment and the help they need as soon as possible.

Carers have a tremendous influence on a young person's attitude towards reading and writing. Remind them that everybody is good at something and even though they may find reading and writing difficult, they may have other strengths.

It is important to understand the difficulties dyslexic young people have in the classroom. In addition to the problems they have with reading, writing and spelling, they may not be able to remember instructions or organise themselves or their ideas in a piece of written work. This often means that they think they are no good at school work.

Some ideas to help a dyslexic young person
Reading
Be prepared for the fact that as your young person becomes older, they may see reading as less important. It may be a lower priority than finishing off the large amounts of homework that they will receive.

Give lots of praise
- Help with reading textbooks, worksheets etc, when requested.
- Help them learn key words for the unit of work being covered.
- Encourage reading a variety of materials – comics, magazines, car or bike manuals etc.

But most of all, regardless of the age – make reading fun and enjoyable!

Spelling
- Encourage the use of a simple dictionary.
- Encourage the use of a spellchecker on the computer but make sure it is set up for English spelling.
- Encourage the use of a key word list – place this in a pocket at the front or back of the exercise book concerned or anywhere else that might help.
- Encourage them to look through their work and try to identify words that are spelled incorrectly or that they are not sure about.
- Test your young person on difficult words if they will accept this. Remember they should always write the words down.
- Look through newspapers and magazines highlighting specific words.

Writing
- Encourage the young person to have a well-stocked pencil case – sharp pencils, eraser, pencil sharpener, highlighters, ruler, etc. Their handwriting may look better by using a fibre tipped pen with blue ink.
- Encourage them to continue with the good writing habits formed at primary school – joined up writing, correct writing position.

Organisation and study skills
Encourage them to use charts, timetables, weekly planner or diary to record such things as PE kit needed or to buy food for a particular session. Good communication between home and school is also important to help them meet deadlines and understand what needs to be done. Also decide between you on a place near the front door for their schoolwork; their school bag; other things needed for school; signed permission slips; lunch money and PE kit.

Computers
Word processing is really helpful for young people who are dyslexic as it is easier and quicker; it looks good, changes to order can be made easily and mistakes edited. Spellcheckers can be a great help but they won't spot the wrong use of 'there' or 'their' for example.

Attachment disorder

It is well researched that some young people's emotional development is interrupted in their early years. This causes great problems to them in forming and maintaining relationships. In an 'ordinary' family, bonding and attachment happens quite naturally. From this interaction of adult and young person comes a sense of trust and security for the young person. Young people in care may have missed this bonding. All these early life experiences may impact greatly on a young person's ability to learn.

Specific needs of young people with attachment disorder:
- To be able to respond positively to another person and to understand the 'normal' rules of life.
- To respond with reasonable requests and to have a realistic sense of themselves.
- To learn to get on with others and to accept responsibility for their own actions.
- To feel valued.
- To fit into and accept the family and school dynamics.
- To manage temper and anger appropriately.
- To understand the world around him/her.
- To understand their own wants, needs and feelings
- To have a sense of their own identity.

Meeting the needs:
- Provide a positive role model to whom the young person can relate.
- Give clear, consistent guidelines and boundaries, but allow some flexibility.
- Be as honest and truthful as possible, with sensitivity to the young person's feelings – give calm, measured responses in confrontational situations.
- Create win win situations.
- Always endeavour to let them know it is their behaviour that isn't liked, not them.
- Tell them what behaviours annoy or irritate, and tell them why. They can't change behaviours they do not recognise as causing problems.

- Allow your emotions (anger, frustration, sadness, happiness, etc.) to be seen appropriately: parents and carers are people too.
- Confront feelings in an open, honest way and help to build positive relationships – anticipate their behaviours; let them know you are doing this.
- Have a good working relationship with families, parents, social workers etc. to address the learning process through psychotherapy, counselling, etc.
- Listen to the young person: hear what they have to say. But remember, they communicate in more ways than just verbally.
- Plan with them for their life; help them to understand the attachment process and how they can be positive in the role as adult.
- Remember that the adult is responsible for helping the young person make appropriate, positive attachments.
- Give them a safe, secure environment to express their feelings, fears, hurt, etc.

Attention deficit hyperactivity disorder (ADHD)

ADHD is a condition where the young person (in comparison to most young people of the same age and sex) has a significantly reduced ability to:
- Maintain attention.
- Control doing or saying something by thinking first (impulsivity).
- Regulate the amount of physical activity according to the situation.
- Be motivated to listen to those in authority and to act on what they have been told.

Attention deficit disorder (ADD)

This is similar to ADHD but the young person normally has the ability to sit or stay still. In a group of 20-30 young people there will probably be at least one ADHD sufferer. It is three times more common in boys than girls.

Supporting young people with ADHD or ADD
- The young person may need support that is multi-disciplinary – medical, psychological, educational and behavioural.
- Parents and carers may need support to deal with issues within the family so people understand the young person is not being naughty or lazy.
- Behaviour modification – see Section 8.
- Give short clear instructions.
- Avoid repetitive tasks.
- Academic targets are more effective than behaviour such as sitting in a seat.
- Give praise.
- Negative comments should be followed by a focus on the desired behaviour.
- Preview tasks so that the young person knows what is expected of them.
- Working one-to-one is more effective than working with groups.
- Sitting where there is less likely to be frequent distractions is useful.
- Alternative ways of presenting information can be helpful.
- Medication – sometimes people are keen for the young person to be given medication before trying to help them in other ways first. Medication should only be given as a last resort, when other ways of helping the young person have been tried without success. Any medication, such as Ritalin, should be given exactly as directed and for as short a period as possible as it may have side effects.

Autistic spectrum condition (Autism)

Young people with autistic spectrum continuum (usually know as autism) exhibit, to a greater or lesser degree, the following three areas of impairment which are the defining characteristic of autism:

- Communication: Language impairment across all types of communication: speech, intonation, gesture, facial expression and other body language.
- Imagination: Rigidity and inflexibility of thought process: resistance to change, obsessional and ritualistic behaviour.
- Socialisation: Difficulties with social relationships, poor social timing, lack of social empathy, rejection of normal body contact, inappropriate eye contact.

Autism is not a new disorder. There have been references to people who appear to have had the condition throughout history.

When helping a young person with autism, priority should be given to self care skills. These will not be learnt without specific teaching. Most young people with autism can learn to carry out all normal household tasks and these skills will be useful to them throughout life. Young people will need to be taught a wide range of social skills which the rest of us take for granted, such as:

- How to hold a conversation.
- That we all have thoughts and emotions.
- That other people have a point of view.

In school, most young people with autism can benefit from normal lessons provided care is taken in making it accessible for them. Unless a wide range of activities is offered to the young person there will be no way of knowing what skills they may be able to develop. Some show ability which far outstrips their general ability levels, e.g. in maths or remembering historical facts and figures.

They often have poor movement skills. They do not understand team games and rules. Playing active sports as well as games such as dominoes and board games is helpful as they require taking turns and sharing.

Dyspraxia or motor co-ordination disorder (MCD)

Dyspraxia can be diagnosed and the physical signs can be clearly seen in situations where balance, motor planning and co-ordination are needed, such as in physical education lessons. The young person may exhibit one or more of the following:

- Movements which are too fast.
- Movements which are too slow.
- Movements which are lacking in control.
- Very slow to process information and pick up external signals.
- Constant fidgeting – moving arms and legs, tapping feet, touching face. These last two may be the result of the effort involved in controlling the body: the pressures required to do this will result in more nervous energy, released by fiddling and fidgeting. These movements are particularly noticeable during formal occasions where the young person is required to sit still, e.g. during assembly, or while watching TV.

- Disjointed movement and speech can become a source of worry, depression and frustration, resulting in behavioural problems caused by stress from constantly having to monitor the body's position and concentrate on communication techniques.
- Difficulty in responding to and carrying out instructions. They may appear to be absorbed in other activities and thus ignoring instructions.
- Difficulty in organising, getting books out, taking messages, getting changed for PE etc, deciding on the correct behaviour in a particular situation.
- Confusion with time – past, present and future. Recall of events may cause major problems. The young person may find the recalling of the correct word a problem, and may go off at a tangent, talking about something totally unrelated.
- Disruptive behaviour. Within a class or family group, the young person may have the attention of a butterfly, darting from one thing to another. The young person may play with anything they can find, and their actions may seem to have no regard for the consequences. On other occasions the young person may be totally absorbed to the exclusion of all else, verbal instructions included.
- Difficulty in thinking through a plan of action. The young person may not be capable of processing information in logical order.
- These young people may behave on the spur of the moment. This can have repercussions within a peer or sibling group. The young person might find him or herself set up as a victim of teasing or bullying in order to provoke an instant reaction.
- To write neatly will demand tremendous muscle control.

Young people with disabilities

The above information may relate to all young people. However, young people with disabilities will have additional and different educational needs. Definitions of disability should not be completely based on 'diagnosis' or 'impairment', but take into account the impact of the impairment on the young person's life and the life of their family.

The aim of the school should be to help the young person make informed choices about their lives. Disabled young people may have a huge number of professionals involved with them. They must know who they are and if there are changes these should be explained - physiotherapist, speech and language therapist, taxi driver, escort. The biggest source of help and support, apart from the carer or the young person's family, will come through schools. They can offer a range of communication support including sign language.

Disabled young people in care should all have a PEP and some specialist resources may be necessary depending on the level of disability and behaviour of the young person. The social worker and teacher will be involved in this and the young person will be consulted if this is possible. There may also be contact with parents, carers, health office staff and support assistants.

Some disabled young people will achieve academically as well as any other young person. However, others will reach level P – pre-curriculum. On the PEP there is space for awards, achievements plus extra curricular activities.

Careers

Every young person is entitled to support from a named personal tutor who can give high-quality impartial careers education and direct insights into the world of work. Ask at school, at the education office or visit a careers office in your area or you can visit the web site, www.careersdirect.org.uk

Part-time jobs

? *Can I have a part-time job?*

Yes, when you are 13 or 14 depending on the area where you live. But you may need a work permit until you are 16. Some local authorities may do things differently, but the principle is the same.

? *Why should I have a work permit?*

To make sure that:
- You are covered by insurance if you have an accident.
- The employer obeys the law.

? *How do I get a work permit?*

A young person can get a form from their new employer, from their school, or from the education office.

? *What do I do with the form?*

Make sure that every part of the form is filled in, and that the employer sends it to the address shown on the form before you start work. You will be sent an employment card which you must keep in case an inspector asks to see it.

? *What sort of work can and can't I do?*

The number of hours and the days on which a young person can work vary according to age and term/non-term time. See www.direct.gov.uk/en/YoungPeople/Workandcareers/index.htm

No person under 16 or who is of compulsory school age can work:
- in a quarry or a mine
- in a factory
- in the transport industry
- collecting or sorting refuse
- in a fish shop
- in delivering milk
- on a building site
- in telephone sales or canvassing
- making house to house collections

Young people can't serve alcohol or petrol until they are 18.

Babysitting is not classed as employment.

Apprenticeships

For those who do not wish to attend college full time apprenticeships are an excellent way of working, earning and studying at the same time. There are different types of apprenticeships suitable for young people with different levels of ability/qualifications. Places are short so early applications are important. Contact the careers adviser or go on line to find more details.

Glossary of terms

NEET

NEET stands for not in education, employment or training. There are many initiatives to try to ensure that no young person has the label of NEET. Find out all you can about what help, assistance and guidance is available in your area so that you can support the young person in every way you can.

Individual Education Plans (IEP)

Individual Education Plans may be produced if the young person has been in trouble or is getting behind with their work. The five stage process is as follows:

1. Identify the problem.
2. Agree with everyone, including the young person, the action, activities and resources needed.
3. Decide on parent or carer support.
4. Set targets and timescales.
5. Monitor and review.

Personal Education Plans (PEP)

Personal Education Plans are compulsory for every young person who is in care. It should be produced immediately they start school and stays with them during the whole of their school career. If the young person moves schools this should come with them and move with them to the next school. It should NOT be confused with an IEP. The aim is to ensure that all those involved with the young person know:

- The young person's level of achievement.
- Any specific learning difficulties.
- Any extra help needed to enable them to catch up.
- Their plans for the future and the school's plans for the young person.

The document is kept by the school and reviewed annually or earlier if appropriate.

Designated teachers

Designated teachers are allocated to every young person in care and young people should be told who their designated teacher is. This person is responsible for the production of the PEP and for handling any difficulties or problems that may arise relating to the young person

Special Education Needs Co-ordinators (SENCO)

Special Education Needs Co-ordinators must be appointed in every school and should have knowledge and understanding of young people with special education needs. They will be responsible for drawing up appropriate plans for the whole school and for ensuring these are implemented. In this way all young people should have the best life chances possible.

Statements of Special Educational Needs ('Records' in Scotland)

Statements of Special Educational Needs may be made about a young person who has special education needs, which will ensure that they get additional help to support them during their school career. These statements are reviewed regularly and they act as a guide to all concerned in improving the life chances of these young people. It is a six-part document provided by the local education authority that covers:

- The young person's personal details.
- The young person's special educational needs.
- Provision available for those with special educational needs.
- Type and name of school.
- Non educational needs (usually involving the health authority).
- Non educational provision (e.g. speech therapy).

The following are normally included:

- The development of the young person in all ways, physical, linguistic and social as well as educational.
- Any special weaknesses and gaps which may hamper progress, e.g. problems with memory.
- What improvements are hoped for.
- How these hoped for improvements can be made including any specialised equipment, facilities and extra teaching necessary.

Different types of schools

Mainstream schools

These are attended by young people who are developing at the normal pattern and rate for their age. Young people with special educational needs should also attend mainstream schools if possible. Many schools integrate all young people in the same schools using classroom assistants where necessary. Where the parents request this, every effort must be made to accommodate the young person in the school. Some of these young people will have a statement which sets down the extra support that the school must give that young person (see above). Some mainstream schools have units attached to them. These units and the reason a young person attends them vary considerably from one local education authority to another; you will need to check locally. The reasons for a young person attending a unit should be clearly stated.

Sometimes what is best for the young person is not available. Make a nuisance of yourself, keep plugging away until you are satisfied that the young person is getting the education to which they are entitled. It is very easy to accept what people in authority say. If you are not satisfied, say so. It really is worth sticking out for what you know is best for the young person.

Units

The young people in a unit will have specific difficulties and their needs will be judged to be too great to place them in a mainstream school even with extra support. The aim is to return the young person to mainstream education as soon as possible. In these units young people usually work in smaller groups and have individual programmes which give them the particular extra help they need and for which they might be statemented. In some units the young people are with the mainstream school whenever possible, e.g. playtimes, mealtimes, possibly in art or drama lessons.

Each unit and school will have a system that is best suited to the particular young person's needs.

Behaviour units are where young people attend when it is not possible to control their behaviour within a school. Young people learn anger management and other behaviour techniques as well as normal lessons. This usually enables them to return to their usual classroom in the future.

Language centres are for young people who may have language problems or delays. In some local education authority areas, young people's non-verbal skills will need to be at least age-appropriate. In others, young people with a language problem and another problem, e.g. behaviour, may be considered for entry. Again, integration with mainstream schools where possible is encouraged.

Diagnostic units are where young people attend so that specialists can have a chance to watch them and find out what the problems are and suggest the best ways for helping them.

Other units exist, for instance for hearing impaired pupils. Most young people can have their needs met locally or by being taxied or bussed to a specialist unit or school, however, 'out-of-county' provision sometimes needs to be made. In very severe cases this could involve weekly boarding or even attendance at a non-local authority school, such as those run by the National Autistic Society. In rare cases a young person may go to a boarding school for 52 weeks a year.

There are other types of school a young person may attend if they have:
- Moderate learning difficulties (MLD).
- Physical difficulties (PD).
- Severe learning difficulties (SLD).
- Profound multiple learning difficulties (PMLD).
- Emotional and behavioural difficulties (EBD).

All authorities have different guidelines for attendance at these schools. Check that you know exactly why the young person is attending a particular school and what you can do to help. Find out when the young person will be able to attend mainstream school.

Some of these terms may vary from place to place but the over-riding principle is the same.

Special educational provision
This means providing help that is extra or different from what is generally available.

The chapter is based on material gathered from a series of wide ranging discussions that were undertaken with people of all ages in order to elicit their attitudes to diversity and to try to understand how these impact on themselves and on others.

Diversity is understood to include race or ethnic origin, religion, culture, sex, sexual orientation, age, nationality, disability, social class and language. This section does not discuss other people's faiths, beliefs or traditions explicitly but tries to work through the complex web of attitudes, experiences and values. The aim is to help young people to value and celebrate diversity and yet retain their own sense of self. At the end of the chapter there is a brief summary of the religions most commonly practised in the UK today.

The first part of the chapter looks at religion and spirituality and how some of the issues highlighted later in the chapter have their foundations in religion, such as the attitude to women and homosexuality. It also looks at race, nationality, ethnic origin and culture before moving on to deal with diverse sexuality.

Religion and spirituality

Children and young people have a right to learn about religious and secular ways of life in an unbiased, non-judgmental way, as Hassan says in *Who am I, Who are you?* (Jenny Nemko, 2006, published by Russell House Publishing.)

> *We need to develop mutual knowledge, not just tolerance. The question is, what are you doing to find out about others? Respect comes out of knowledge; when you recognize my reality is as complex as yours, that's when you begin to know me and respect me.*

Children's right to spiritual and religious development is not only enshrined in the UN Convention on the Rights of the Child under article 27, but also in UK legislation and government guidance such as The Education Reform Act 1988; the National Minimum Standards (England and Wales) and various Children Acts across the UK.

Spirituality is about understanding oneself, which may change as circumstances change. It is about developing one's own ideas and beliefs on morality, ethics, behaviour, love, life, death, happiness, values, standards and so on. Many people join established religions where they meet people with similar beliefs and partake in acts of worship.

There are other groups that people join that are not immediately thought of as religions. For example:

- Spiritualism lets you define God in your own personal way. It does not dictate that God be a person on a throne or even a person at all, the definition of God is personally yours.
- Postmodernism is a view of religion without God.
- People may also call themselves Atheists as they do not believe that God exists.
- Agnostics suggest that it is impossible to prove that god exists.
- There are also Humanists and many other groups including those that believe in the paranormal.

Within each religion, there are likely to be different beliefs and levels of commitment. People from different countries or different parts of the same country may behave in slightly different ways and have slightly different beliefs and customs for the same religion.

A true story

There is a man called John but he is called 'Jock' because he is Scottish and very proud of his heritage. He lives in England but is the most 'Scottish' person anyone knows. At every opportunity he wears his kilt, he speaks with an extremely broad Scottish accent, eats only traditional Scottish food. When in Scotland he was a member of the Scottish Presbyterian church which is part of the Christian religion in the UK. Whilst in England he attends the local church as he feels it is his duty to do attend a church but he does not enjoy it because as he says 'they do things differently'.

Everyone loves Jock and thinks he is rather quaint. Yet these same people may think very differently if say a Seikh or a Muslim behaved in this way. People have a right to practice their own religion in their own way but have a responsibility to be tolerant of other people's beliefs and religion.

A religion needs continuity and rules to give it strength. It also needs to grow and change to reflect the ideas and needs of a new generation in an ever changing world. We all need to be understanding and respectful of each other's religions, customs, symbols and places of worship.

All religions however have certain over-riding principles which basically are:
- Not to lie, cheat, or steal.
- To be kind to people, to help them and not to fight.
- To share things.
- To look after their family and other people close to them.

Many people who do not believe in any religion still believe in the above and try to be a good person.

In order to better understand diversity, children and young people should be helped to find out:
- what different people believe and think
- what they eat and don't eat
- what they should and shouldn't do
- what they should wear and where they should go

Young people have a right to make their own informed decisions about their religion and beliefs whilst at the same time respecting the decisions of others.

Race, nationality, ethnic origin and culture

"In my culture..."   *"no, in my culture...."*   *"no, no, no...."*

The above were comments made during a discussion with young people showing the lack of knowledge of the different individuals. The whole issue is so important that it should be discussed openly with accurate information readily available to help young people to mutually understand each other's beliefs and way of life.

Young people often have their own ideas about race and culture. They probably fall into three groups. Firstly, those who only wish to mix with people of the same race, who are exceptionally aware of all racial issues and whose racial ties are strong; secondly, young people who are not sure how they wish to be seen and are somewhat confused about race issues; and thirdly those who wish to be known and treated as British (this may be especially true of young people who were born and bred in the UK).

At a social work conference there was a group of young people at the front on the stage. At question time, one social worker asked them if they could give examples of racial prejudice that had affected them. The two Asian girls and the three black boys could not think of anything. Then one of the white girls said 'yes, I am Irish and people think I'm thick and eat fish on Fridays'.

This was clearly not the response expected or even wanted. We have a situation in the UK at present where there are competing views as to what constitutes racial discrimination. There are people from specific groups who have become so vociferous that their views sometimes override all other views. There are also people who are so afraid to say what they think in case they are accused of racism that they say nothing even when what they see or observe is inappropriate.

Trevor, a teenager said:

> Although I'm proud of my heritage and would one day like to go to see where I came from, I'm sick and tired of being told I'm black and of people treating me differently. I am British, I was born in Britain and I want to be treated like other British people. I don't want special or different treatment just because I am black.

Every young person has the right to be treated fairly and honestly regardless of their differences such as whether they are fat or thin, black or white, wear glasses, has a squint, speaks with a stutter, is deaf or mute, has lived in the UK all their life or has just arrived. Equally they also have a responsibility to treat other people fairly, to respect their views, their culture and their heritage.

One of the difficulties for young people in the UK is that they often want to be just like any other young person but they have divided loyalties. They may have been put under pressure from others to conform to certain standards such as at school because of 'politically correct' attitudes of certain staff members, or at the church that their family attends.

Maria was completing an application form for a part-time job. Her mentor, a white worker, read it through and said:

*"you **must** put 'black' under the question of your origin"*

"why" she replied, *"I'm British, I don't want to get a job or not get it, just because I'm black"*

Some young people, in their teenage years particularly, may become almost obsessed with all things relating to their race. They wear the clothes, speak or learn the language of their heritage and join like-minded groups to the exclusion of others. Certain family members or older people from their religious or political group become a huge influence on their lives and thinking. This is a very natural happening providing they are given opportunities to make their own decisions and develop their own ideas and beliefs.

Symbols that identify our beliefs may cause anxiety and confusion. Wearing a crucifix, covering your legs, wearing a skull cap or veil to cover you face are examples of symbolism which enable the wearer to acknowledge their particular religious belief. However, some people may wear them as a fashion item with no thought for their religious implications. Similarly, there are other things that one is supposed to do or not do, such as not doing work on a Sunday, or eating particular food, which may have originally been grounded in religious beliefs, yet there may be no apparent evidence for this within the holy book of the particular faith.

Symbolism may also be a way of helping someone to cope with a difficult time in their life, as the following example shows:

My father re-married and my step-mother did not show any interest in my sister and me. When he died my step-mother made it clear that she did not wish us to attend the funeral and as I had no wish to cause an argument, I did not attend. I spent the day of the funeral in a state of limbo, not able to settle or knowing what to do. Eventually, my gran suggested that I should buy a plant and put it in her garden in memory of my dad. The amazing thing was that once we had planted the bush I felt totally calm and at peace with myself.

Molly, a teenager

The whole notion of an 'arranged' marriage for young girls but also for boys, is another area where the rights of the young person may not be considered. Sometimes these young people, in order to not upset their family, marry their parents' choice. This person then takes them to live with a family they do not know, often many miles away. There are differences between an arranged marriage and a forced marriage but both are wrong if there is no right of choice. Girls and boys can be forced into marriage at a very young age which actually contravenes their faith but which has happened for so long within their community and culture that everyone accepts it, that is except the young people. This practice is more common for girls but it is becoming increasing clear that more boys may also be forced into marriage than had been originally thought.

Children and young people who are of mixed race may be further disadvantaged. The term mixed-race itself can be mis-leading and does not begin to describe their actual ethnicity or heritage. Their skin may be black or it may be white depending on the genes of their parents but their brothers and sisters may have a different colour skin even though they may share a parent. Much has been written about black children in care being brought up by white foster carers but very little seems to have been written about mixed race children.

In some countries the masculinity of men is sometimes based on the number of children they have. This can mean that men have a series of children by different women. It is also, in some families, acceptable for a man to marry and yet still expect to visit his own family regularly and go out with brothers and friends and behave as though he was single. Clearly this is difficult for children of these liaisons to understand. Sometimes the men support the children financially but at other times they may disappear and the women must cope alone. These children may be of a different skin colour to their mother and may not know anything about the culture and way of life of their father, they may not have male role models to help them through life and they may feel marginalised by society.

Sexuality

(See also Section 5 from page 50.)

The age of consent for sex whether hetero-sexual or homo-sexual is 16 years. There are many teenagers who have sex before this, sometimes before they are ready, but they feel peer pressure to conform. Young people should never be enticed or encouraged (certainly never forcibly) to enter into any kind of sexual relationship.

One of the reasons for the high teenage pregnancy rate is the differing attitudes in wider society. Some will talk about relationships and sexual matters freely, others will not; some will provide contraception and family planning advice, others will not; some will help with arranging an abortion, some will not. Young people have the right to be given all the help and advice possible so that they can make their own informed decisions about whether to have a sex with someone or not and whether to have a termination or consider adoption.

Some people will tell you that they knew from a very early age that they were 'different' from other children; they knew they did not like playing traditional boys or girls games; that they preferred wearing the clothes of children of the opposite sex and that as they grew older they were victims of a good deal of ridicule and some times bullying. Clearly this is not right but their treatment by others may be out of ignorance rather than malice.

Other children may have been abused and come to hate people of the opposite sex. As a result they may develop gay tendencies and only feel safe and comfortable in a same sex relationship.

A true story
Karen 'came out' when she joined the sixth form of her local school. She had always been a loner and dressed in a masculine style so no one was surprised when she said she was gay. She was treated well by both staff and other sixth formers. However, ultimately it became clear that she had been abusing her position as a sixth former to entice younger girls to take part in sexual acts with her on the school premises. After a thorough investigation Karen left the school.

There is nothing wrong with same sex relationships, provided they are born from respect, caring and love and not in order to satisfy someone else's sexual pleasure. As in all sexual relationships, young people need to learn to say no, to make their own decisions but in order to be able to do this they need knowledge about different ways of life, different types of relationships and skills to make judgments about their own relationships. Some young people live in households where same sex relationships are the norm, the children being born following a parent's IVF treatment or the parent having decided to admit their sexuality after they have had children. They may be being fostered or have been adopted by same sex couples. These young people, as well as needing the skills mentioned above, also need to be helped to give appropriate responses when they are quizzed by others.

Young people have a right to be protected from bullying but young people who are either gay themselves or have gay parents may be particularly prone to bullying so they may need extra help as well as vigilance from appropriate adults.

Teenagers may sometimes develop bi-sexual tendencies where they are not sure of who they are and where they are going as far as their sexuality is concerned.

We should all try to help young people understand issues around race, religion and culture. We should be looking for tolerance, compassion, understanding and love. By so doing young people can be helped to be themselves whilst understanding other people around them.

The 'PC' (politically correct) lobby is very powerful and it some times, almost subconsciously, feels we should or should not be doing something. PC has come to mean saying or writing something only after care has been taken not to upset anyone in any shape or form. There is no problem with that but generally no one would set out to upset anyone. However, sometimes people's feelings and emotions are not explored because of this so opportunities are missed for discussion or understanding. This cannot be right for anyone, especially children, where teachers, for example, do not fully address the underlying causes of the bullying for fear of saying the wrong thing.

We need to start when children are very young to give them opportunities to learn about other people's faiths, cultures and way of life, gradually moving to having more meaningful debates as young people develop during their teenage years.

Religions

Brief descriptions of some of the religions practised in the UK today follow:

- Buddhism
- Christianity
- Hinduism
- Islam
- Judaism
- Sikhism

Religion means different things to all these groups of people. Within each religion, there are likely to be different sects with different levels of commitment. A religion needs continuity and rules to give it strength. It also needs to grow and change to the ideas and needs of a new generation and an ever changing world. We all need to be understanding and be respectful of each other's religions, customs, symbols and places of worship.

Buddhism

Buddhism is a philosophy, or way of thinking, rather than a set of social rules. Belief in re-incarnation encourages a Buddhist to lead a good life. The name Buddha means 'enlightened one'. There are many Buddhist sects, but all follow the five laws (silas):

- no killing
- no stealing
- no sexual misconduct
- no falsehoods
- no drinking of intoxicating substances

Buddhism shows a love for all living beings and respect for all forms of life. Charity, hospitality and self-discipline are encouraged. The Buddhist goal is to escape the eternal cycle of life and death and to reach a state of perfection – 'Nirvana'.

Religious observances: Buddhists worship in temples in which are huge statues of Buddha. The monks and nuns shave their heads and wear yellow robes.

Buddhist festival: Late May-early June: Wesak.

Worship consists of meditation and chanting. Incense and candles are often burned and flowers offered. Some Buddhists fast on the first and 15th day of each lunar month (between the new and full moon). Fasting may just mean no meat eating, but is a matter of personal choice.

Diet: No regulations; but the majority of Buddhists are vegetarians.

Birth customs: Nothing specific is laid down.

Death: Cremation is preferred.

Christianity

Christianity is named after Jesus Christ who is considered by his followers to be the Son of God, made man, but also God in His own right.

There are many sects of Christians in all countries in the world. As Christianity spread to different parts of the world, each country accepted its main beliefs. Each country added its own culture and way of doing things to the forms of worship that were already established. The result is a world-wide religion and following of people whose beliefs are similar. The only difference is that the ways of worship vary from country to country and even from church to church in the same country. Some Christian churches are Baptist, Catholic, Methodist, Presbyterian, Church of England, Ireland, Scotland and Wales.

As Christ himself was a Jew, the early Christians used a lot of readings from the Old Testament, and psalms and hymns from the Jewish faith.

As Christ's preachings and his follower's letters and accounts of his life were gathered together they formed the 'New Testament'. The 'Old' and 'New' joined together and became known as the Bible or Holy Book of the Christians.

Religious observances: the central beliefs of Christianity are:
- There is only one God – his son, Jesus, died and rose again from the dead.
- The keeping of the Ten Commandments.
- There is resurrection, a life after death, with God for all time.

God consists of three people in one – Father, Son and Holy Spirit.

Some Christians also have a great respect for, but do not worship, Mary, the mother of God or other holy men as Saints

Christians gather in churches to worship. Their holy day is Sunday.

Abortion is not encouraged by the Christian churches. Some, notably the Roman Catholic Church, forbid abortion and birth control.

Diet: No restrictions except on special fast days, e.g. Good Friday for some people.

Birth customs: After birth, Christians are baptised – some shortly after birth, some at an age when they understand what is involved. At baptism a child may be totally immersed in holy water or the sign of the cross may be drawn in holy water on the forehead. Confirmation is when a young person agrees to accept the laws of the church and promises to try to uphold them.

Marriage: Is considered binding but divorce is granted in some circumstances.

Death: A person may be attended by a senior churchgoer, or leader such as a priest or vicar who will be with the person as they near death or as they die. Cremation and burial are both permitted. Christians believe very strongly in the resurrection, or rising again, of the body and soul joined together in God and in eternal life.

Hinduism

Hinduism is the most established of the world's religions. It is not based on the teachings of any one special person. Hinduism is a social system as well as a set of religious beliefs. Hindu practices vary a great deal depending on caste and areas of origin.

Caste is inherited by birth and is determined by individual Karma, meaning reward for good deeds and punishment for wickedness. There are four main groups:
- Brahmin – priestly caste, who teach and perform religious ceremonies and encourage others to learn religious duties.
- Kshatriya – military caste, who protect society and govern, rule and administer a country to lead a disciplined life.
- Vaishya – who engage in business, trade, commerce and agriculture.
- Shudra – the manual labourers.

Hindus in Britain may observe the caste system and wish to avoid dining or inter-marriage with members of other castes.

The five main rules or principles for Hinduism are known as the five 'P's, which translated mean:

1. God
2. Prayer
3. Re-birth
4. Law of action
5. Compassion for all living things

The four things to work for are:
- religious duties
- satisfaction of desire
- material prosperity
- salvation

Religious observances: Hindus pray twice daily. They may use holy books, prayer beads and burn incense. At home a shrine may be set up sometimes in a room set aside for prayer. The temples are used for festivals and special celebrations. Horoscopes are an important part of religious belief. Fasting is practised by devout Hindus, mainly women. Some Hindus may fast weekly, depending on their loyalty to a particular deity or the position of the stars. Fasting to Hindus means eating only pure foods such as fruit or yoghurt.

Diet: Many Hindus are vegetarian. As cows are sacred and pigs are scavenging animals in India, beef and pork are never eaten by Hindus. Some do not eat eggs – they are seen as a source of life – or cheese if it is made with animal rennet. Onions and garlic are seen as harmful stimulants. Some Hindus avoid tea and coffee. Alcohol is officially frowned upon.

Special customs: Spiritual purity and physical cleanliness are extremely important. Most Hindus prefer showers to baths. Modest dress is favoured for both men and women. Women may wear a Sari, loose fitting trousers, a top and a long scarf covering the head (chadar). Men must cover themselves from waist to knee. Women would not expect to undress fully for a medical examination and would prefer to be examined by female medical staff.

Gold worn next to the skin is believed to protect the wearer from many diseases. Married women traditionally wear a gold brooch and bangles. They usually wear a small coloured, red 'bindi' or spot on their foreheads. They may also put red along the parting of their hair in the early years of marriage. Men of the Brahmin caste may wear a holy thread (janeu) over the right shoulder and round the body. It is both religiously and culturally very important and most men would be reluctant to remove it.

Birth: After birth the holy symbol 'Om' is written in honey on the baby's tongue by a close relative. The baby's horoscope is read and the birth celebrated six days later.

Family planning: No specific ruling. Abortion is frowned upon, but individual attitudes vary. Some Hindu women prefer not to leave the home for 40 days after giving birth.

Death: Cremation is preferred.

Traditional medicine: 'Ayurvedic' practice is complementary to conventional health care. The practitioners are known as 'vaids'.

Islam

Muslims believe in one God. They accept all Christian prophets and the old and the new Testament but recognise the prophet Mohammed (PBUH) as *the* prophet. The Prophet's name is always followed by the words 'Peace be upon him' or PBUH.

Religious observances: Worship is in a Mosque but can equally be at home in any place facing towards Mecca. The holy book is called the Koran and Friday is the Muslim's holy day. Islam has no caste system, it is a belief intended for everyone. Muslims are required to:

- Pray five times a day – prayers are preceded by ritual ablutions or washings.
- Fast from dawn to sunset for one lunar month each year. This is known as Ramadan and is a moveable period. Fasting is waived for menstruating, pregnant and breast-feeding women; children who have not reached puberty; people who are ill or on a journey. In the last case, the lost days must be made up later.
- Give two and a half percent of their savings for the needy.
- Make a pilgrimage, or journey, to Mecca, the Holy City, once in their lifetime if health and money permit.

Muslims should wash hands, face and feet in running water before prayer whenever possible. Care should be taken that the toilet itself is not facing Mecca – the south-east, as this would be seen to be disrespectful. Muslims pray facing Mecca and prefer to have a special room set aside for prayer. Shoes are not worn in this room.

Diet: Muslims may not eat the flesh of pigs. Other meat may be eaten provided it is killed in the manner laid down by Islamic law. This meat is called Halal. There are special butchers where this meat is sold. Halal food should not be stored or cooked with non-Halal food. The cooking of Halal foods should be in separate containers. All alcoholic drinks or dishes containing alcohol are forbidden, as are tobacco and drugs.

Special customs: These may vary according to area and degree of adherence to tradition.

Dress: Men must be covered from navel to knee; only the hands and face of women should be seen.

Girls after puberty may cover their heads or wear a veil in school, college or workplace. Sexes may be kept apart until marriage; single sex education is preferred.

Pre-marital and extra-marital sexual relationships are forbidden. Mothers giving birth outside marriage are liable to be rejected by the community. Nakedness is considered shameful. Medical treatment by a person of the same sex is preferred.

Some Muslim cultures may be extremely liberal and it may not be possible to discern someone is a Muslim as they may not dress and act in any way that would indicate their religion. They may also not consider that strict religious observance is necessary.

Birth customs: The Azan, or call to prayer, is recited after the birth.

Family planning: There is no specific Islamic ruling against contraception, but it is disapproved of by some cultures. Abortion is frowned upon, but tolerated for medical reasons.

Male circumcision: All Muslim boys must be circumcised before puberty, any time from eight days to eight years, according to local custom.

Female circumcision: Although practised in some Muslim countries, is not a Muslim religious practice.

Death: A dying Muslim should be turned to face Mecca (south-east). The Koran is read aloud. After death, because the body is considered to be the property of Allah, it must be in the care of Muslims. After washing, the body is dressed in a white shroud. The body must be buried in a Muslim cemetery 24 hours after death. Cremation is forbidden. The anniversary of the death is marked by giving alms to the needy on behalf of the dead person.

Medicine: Some traditional herbal medicines and medical practices are used together with conventional health care by some Muslims.

Judaism

The word God is never written in full in Judaism. Hebrew is the language of prayer. A Rabbi is a Jewish leader, priest and teacher. The Jewish community considers itself to be both a religious community and an ethnic group.

Religious observances: Jewish practices are laid down by the Torah in the Talmud, which are the first five books of the Bible as interpreted by rabbis.

There are different groups of Jews – Orthodox, Reform and Liberal – all of whom observe these rules in different ways:
- The Sabbath or Jewish Holy Day, starts at sunset on Friday and ends on Saturday evening. Orthodox is very strict. Orthodox Jews may not do any kind of work on the Sabbath, not even switching on a light or electrical equipment, driving or using public transport; cooking, telephoning or writing – unless any of these is necessary to save life.
- Fasting for 25 hours beginning at sunset on the eve of Yom Kippur (Day of Atonement); and other specified days.
- Circumcision – nearly all Jewish boys are circumcised by a qualified Mohel eight days after birth.
- At the age of 13 boys are accepted as full members of the community in a ceremony known as Bar Mitzvah. Girls are accepted at the age of 12 with a Bat Mitzvah.

Dress: Modesty is an important religious issue. Orthodox men keep their heads covered with a skull cap (Kappel) and the strictly Orthodox Jews wear a prayer shawl. Phylacteries (small, leather boxes containing biblical texts) are also worn except on the Sabbath. Women wear sleeves below the elbow and hemlines below the knee. They may also wear a scarf or wig (scheitel) in public. Children after the age of eleven should be educated in single sex schools. Hasidic men will not shake hands with women and prefer not to look at them or speak to them.

Diet: These laws are observed to varying degrees by all practising Jews:
- The very religious will not eat before morning prayers, which may take up to 30 minutes.
- Pork and all things made with it are forbidden; so are shellfish, rabbits and birds of prey and some cheeses.
- Kosher is a word used to describe meat that has been killed and prepared according to Jewish law; or to any allowed food, e.g. all fruit and vegetables.
- Orthodox Jews are not permitted to eat meat and dairy products within several hours of each other and must use separate plates and utensils. Orthodox Jews must not take non-kosher medication unless there is no alternative.
- For the eight days of Pesach (Passover) no leavened bread, cakes or biscuits are eaten.

Birth customs: Childbirth is always considered a life-threatening situation. After the head has been delivered the child is considered to be a separate human being whose life may not be sacrificed even to save the mother's life.

Family planning: Some orthodox Jews forbid contraception and abortion unless the mother's health is at risk. Mothers are excused fasting for seven days from the onset of childbirth. Until the 30th day they only have to fast on Yom Kippur (provided they are well).

Death: Jews must be buried on the day of death or as soon as possible afterwards. Cremation is forbidden by Orthodox Jews.

Sikhism

Religious observances: Sikhs or learners were remakers of combined aspects of Islam and Hinduism. They originated in Punjab, India in the 15th Century. Guru Nanak was their leader and with his nine successors is revered as a saint. The Sikh Holy Book is called the Guru Granth Sahib. Sikhs worship together in temples. The most famous of these is the Golden Temple at Amritsar. The river Ganges is held to be a sacred river. Sikh homes may have a shrine for the Holy Book. This may be in a special room. If so, shoes should not be worn in this area and the head should be covered. Prayers are said around sunrise and sunset. Saihajdhari are Sikhs who are striving towards Baptism. Amritdhari (baptised) Sikhs are very strict about diet, dress and prayers.

Dress: Amritdhari have a strict code of dress, known as the five Ks – in translation these mean:
- Cutting of hair is forbidden.
- A comb secures the hair.
- Men wear a turban; women keep their hair covered.
- A metal bangle is worn on the right wrist. A small symbolic dagger is carried.
- Men wear short under-breeches.

Sikh men should not be asked to remove their turbans. Girls should be provided with Shalwar (or loose fitting trousers) instead of skirts and track suits for PE. They may not be permitted to go swimming after the age of 12 years.

Diet: Beef, alcohol and tobacco are forbidden. So is Halal meat. Chicken, lamb or pork may be eaten. The animals should be killed according to Sikh rites (Chattaka). Many Sikhs are vegetarian.

Birth: Is celebrated by a thanksgiving at the temple. After 13 days the baby may be baptised into the order of Khalsa by five Sikhs in the presence of the Holy Books, at home or in the temple. Sweets are given out to celebrate a boy's birth. Mothers are required to rest for 40 days after childbirth and are given rich food. They are forbidden to prepare food during these 40 days.

Death: Readings from the holy book are given by a reader from the local temple or a relative. Non-Sikhs may help the family to lay out the body if asked to do so, but the family is considered responsible for these rites. Cremation is mandatory. The ashes are sprinkled on running water; in India the river Ganges would be considered the best.

Section 8
Personal Development

Growing up

Probably the most difficult phase of our lives is our teens. Do you remember having spots and big feet, developing breasts, having greasy hair, wearing clothes that didn't suit you, blushing, having a crush on a teacher?

The following section covers some of the topics which young people being looked after have asked for help with. These include:

- decision making
- discipline and punishment
- privacy and confidentiality
- self-respect and confidence
- values
- listening and being listened to
- coping with crisis
- worries

Provide them with a happy, warm, caring environment where they can talk about worries openly, have their own privacy and a place to entertain their friends and 'those terrible teenage years' will not be so bad at all.

I think a good carer is someone who sits down and listens to you…
and someone who will follow it through and try to sort out the problem.   young person

You can talk to your foster carer and get an honest answer.   young person

The most valuable thing you can give a young person growing up is your time. Time to listen, time to talk, time to communicate, time to understand.

Growing up is particularly difficult; they'll need all the help and support you can give them.

Decision making

We all know it's much easier to put off making decisions until tomorrow. Decision making is an important life skill which young people need to be taught. They need to learn to make good decisions so that when they are no longer being looked after, making decisions will be a natural thing to do. Hopefully young people won't rush into things but look at the situation from every angle, exploring the options before they decide.

There is pressure on children to make decisions they are not equipped to make.

foster carer

Let them start with simple decisions at first like choosing menus, helping choose holidays, outings, subjects at school, colour schemes, even if it is much easier for you to make the decisions yourself.

Decision-making methods

The following are three ways that could be used to help the decision-making process. You could work through them with young people on a few minor issues at first, either one-to-one or as a group.

1 Simple logical method

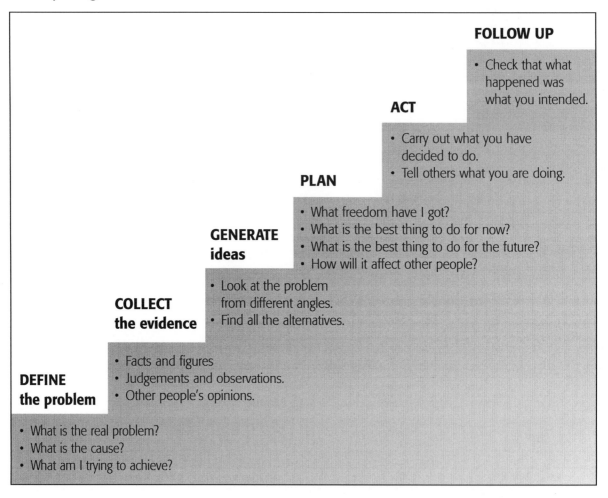

2 For and against (pros and cons) method

Make a list of all the good points and all the bad points of making a decision. It is surprising when you have done this how easy the decision making will be. Compare the 'fors' and 'againsts' as in the following example:

Choice	For	Against
Staying on at same school in 6th form		
Going to local college		
Going to college in next town		

3 Rating method

Decision making using ratings means that you look at the options and then give each option a value. In this way you can work out what each option really means to you:

1. Write down the option or choices at the top of the columns marked X, Y, Z. More columns can be added if needed.
2. Write down all the factors that you want to consider in the column marked **Requirements**, usually about 10 points.
3. Rate the factors from 1 to 10 (10 being the most important and 1 the least important). Put these numbers in the column marked **Rating (A)**. This will show the overall importance to you of the various factors.
4. Give X, Y, Z a mark out of 10 to show how well they meet the **Requirements**. Write the mark in column **(B)**. This will show the difference between each option.
5. Multiply the figure in column **(A)** by the figure in column **(B)** and put your answer in column **(C)**. Do this for each option.
6. Add up all the scores in each column **(C)**. The highest score will be the best option.

Below is an example of a completed rating form. Over the page is a blank one which can be photocopied and used again and again.

REQUIREMENTS	RATING A	Option/choice (all answers out of 10)					
		X Staying on at school in 6th form		Y Going to local college		Z Going to college in next town	
		B	C	B	C	B	C
Choice of subjects	10	7	70	9	90	8	80
Travelling time	4	8	32	5	20	3	12
Travel costs	9	9	81	4	36	8	72
Having friends there	5	10	50	2	10	10	50
Good exam pass rate	8	6	48	8	64	9	72
Good sports facilities	6	10	60	6	36	10	60
Library	2	2	4	3	6	4	8
Good social life	7	3	21	5	35	7	49
Nearness to shops	1	1	1	1	1	3	3
Good canteen	3	1	3	3	9	8	24
Total			370		307		430

REQUIREMENTS	RATING A	Option/choice (all answers out of 10)					
		X		Y		Z	
		B	C	B	C	B	C

Of course, it may be that once you start putting a value on the requirements they seem less important and you will want to change them.

Encouraging positive behaviour

Behaviour is a way of communicating. With some young people being difficult may be their way, often their only way, of telling you that they feel awful, angry or distressed about something or everything. Extreme behaviour is often related to extreme distress.

When a young person has been particularly difficult, especially if this behaviour comes out of the blue, try to find out what is bothering them – not, of course, until they have calmed down. If the young person is reluctant to talk, you might find the section on worries (pages 122-123) helpful.

It is a good idea to make a note of when difficult behaviour occurs to see if there is a pattern. For example, a young person may be 'high' say every Tuesday, after school (because, for example, they 'hate' the teacher of a particular subject). Someone else may be difficult after reviews or visits home. You can then make your own plans of how to prevent problems occurring.

It is also worth noting when they are not being difficult. You can then speak to them positively and get them to notice this for themselves.

This sort of analysis is called the ABC analysis.
- **A Antecedent** – what happens before the behaviour
- **B Behaviour** – what actually happens
- **C Consequence** – what happens as a result of the behaviour

It is equally useful for positive behaviour as well as for difficult behaviour as it helps build a picture of the young person's behaviour patterns and will help you to take action accordingly.

Be aware of what is going on in the home. It may be possible to diffuse a situation just by being in the room, or in a doorway or in the garden.

However, if a situation gets out of control or the young person is likely to harm themselves or others, then carers may, in exceptional circumstances, use minimum physical constraint or lock doors to prevent escape.

Bedroom doors should not be locked at night although occasionally it may be necessary for the carer to be near the bedroom to ensure the young person does not run away.

Carers should:
- Praise positive behaviour.
- Work hard to build a good relationship with the young person.
- Provide them with a good environment, a home they value. If the place looks good and the young people are involved in setting the rules and in decisions that affect the home they will behave much better.

- Involve them in tasks and help them complete them, but make sure the tasks are not too difficult and that they understand what is required. When the going gets tough some young people may give up. Help them to see the task through – you'll be surprised how pleased they will be. They'll have a sense of achievement even with the simplest of jobs.
- Find ways to relieve boredom. Look for ways to stimulate young people.
- Not say 'no' too often but if you do say no, then keep to it.
- Be friendly with the young person. However, they may need to have someone to rebel against and that person will probably be you.
- Be patient. Young people will need to learn to trust you and to know you will trust them. They want to respect you – their behaviour may not always indicate this.
- Try to stay one step ahead of the young person. Plan activities, events, discussions.
- Be ready for possible explosive situations.
- Be around the house, be available for a chat.

The La Vigna model

This is a widely used behaviour management strategy which has five parts. All may be used or only one strategy may be necessary. For example lessening the noise in a room by switching the sound down on the television may cause a complete and sudden change of behaviour in the young person.

The strategies are:

Environment change

Moving the young person to another room or changing the lighting, noise levels, crowding, or temperature.

Time

Giving them time: time alone, your time and other people's time.

New skills

Focusing on why the young person behaves in a particular way and teaching them other ways of achieving the same ends. Ask yourself, and get them to ask themselves, what does this behaviour mean? It may be a coping strategy that the young person has developed over time in response to their experiences, even though it may be an ineffective way of getting their needs met. A new teacher said:

I didn't realise that when a young person said that it was stupid and a waste of time what they really meant was that they couldn't do it or hadn't understood. Once I realised that, I was better able to cope with and avoid these difficult situations.

In this case the young person needs to learn to ask, if not sure. They need to know that to ask is a strength and not a weakness. They also need to learn about the quality and quantity of relationships, respect and dignity and how to express their needs and emotions.

Positive reinforcement

Some young people (and some adults!) think any attention is better than none. Sometimes adults unwittingly reward bad behaviour by giving the young person extra attention. They fail to give reward or recognition to the good behaviour. The young person then feels as though they are being punished for behaving well.

Some tips to positive reinforcement:
- **Notice good behaviour.** This may not be as easy as it sounds particularly if you are having a bad day with a young person. Even if it is something basic, notice that the young person has done something well or right and say so. For instance, *'I know you have been unhappy or had a bad day but I wanted you to know that I saw how well you worked on your homework'*.
- Try this simple rule. For every negative statement you make, or may need to make, to a young person, make six positive ones. If you think you may not be able to find six positive things to say, think why you need to make a negative statement at all and see if this can be said in a positive but still effective way. For instance, instead of telling the young person they have made a mess in the room with their toys and they must tidy up, try saying: *'it looks like you have had a really interesting time. Tell me about it.'* Once you have given the young person time to share with you, you are more likely to get them to co-operate in tidying up.

A summary of positive reinforcement:
- Create opportunities for success or for having fun.
- Create structure and stability for the young person.
- Plan in consistent encouragement – this can be difficult to do but try using the one negative thing to six positives rule above.
- Keep expectations clear, age appropriate and specific.
- Teach new skills and behaviours using encouragement and limit setting.

You can also use a star chart or reward system. There has been much debate regarding the use of rewards. Many people would say that motivation by reward only lasts for a very limited time so other forms of behaviour management are needed. There are many such charts that you can buy or they are easy to make. The important thing to ensure when creating a reward chart is that:
- So far as possible, agree the reason for the chart and have clear expectations for achievement of the reward.
- Ensure you have agreed what the purpose is and what the reward is to be. Don't make it so easy because they need to know they have to make an effort.
- Rewards may need to be graded to ensure that even if the young person does not completely fulfil the expectations, they are rewarded for what effort they have made.
- Such methods can be used short-term: or for a much longer period if, for instance, a young person wishes their reward to be a bike.

Reactive strategies

The previous areas have focused on bringing about positive behaviour changes for the young person. Such a process will not, of course, work overnight. It will take time for the young person to learn new skills and new behaviour patterns. In the meantime, it will be necessary to have planned strategies for responding to unacceptable behaviour. Reactive strategies are not about improvements in behaviour but managing immediate situations in a way which seeks to avoid escalation into more difficult situations. For example:

- Non-verbal signal – *eye contact, frown, glare.*
- Close proximity – *simply moving closer to the young person.*
- Redirection – divert the young person's attention.
- Reward, praise – *'that looks interesting, well done, shall we try'* (comment directly on something positive).
- Active listening – *not assuming you always know what the difficulties are but genuinely listening to the young person's views and reflecting their feelings back to them.*
- Humour – *not sarcasm.*
- Relocating – *suggest they move to another room.*
- Ignoring – *sometimes ignoring the situation is the best strategy but being aware of early signs of escalation is vital.*

To recap, it is possible to reduce inappropriate behaviour by:

- Preventing the behaviour in the first place by arranging the environment so that opportunities for misbehaviour are minimised.
- Seeing what the aim of the problem behaviour is and replacing it by alternative methods that are easier for the young person and socially acceptable.

What a young person should know about their behaviour

As they get older, young people should be encouraged to discuss:

- Their behaviour and others' behaviour.
- Right and wrong.
- What is acceptable and what is not.
- What control is needed and why.
- What sanctions should be imposed, how and by whom. They need to believe the system in their home is fair and is applied across the board consistently.
- Their relationship with carers, teachers and other young people and why they might feel aggressive towards them, frightened of them or impressed by them.

Young people also need to learn to aim for standards they can achieve. It is important that they be responsible for their own behaviour and the consequences of it. Young people must learn to be realistic.

> *I want discipline. At my review I got what I wanted...I had got used to discipline… and there wasn't any. I asked to be disciplined. My brother asked to be disciplined.*
>
> teenager

Young people really do want discipline. They want to know their carers care. They want to know how far they can go and what the consequences will be if they go beyond the boundaries. In many local authority areas the term 'care and control' is used instead of 'discipline and punishment' but young people prefer the terms they know.

What carers should not do
The following forms of punishment are not allowed in children's homes or foster care:
- Corporal (physical) punishment (except in Scotland – where there are strict guidelines) such as slapping, pinching, squeezing, shaking or rough handling. It does not, however, prevent a carer from taking necessary physical action to prevent danger or injury, to themselves or another person, or to avoid damage to property.
- Withholding food, drink and medicines.
- Restricting contact with family or social workers.
- Forcing young people to wear clothing that is unsuitable.
- Depriving young people of sleep.
- Withholding medical or dental treatment.

With regard to punishment, foster carers are given similar powers to parents under the law. They are permitted to enforce 'reasonable' discipline and punishment but they should take the above as guidelines. Carers also have to be sensitive and to know when to hold back. It may, after all, be the first time the young person has really had fun and the offence isn't really that bad anyway! Sometimes it is difficult to understand why a young person behaves in a particular way. For example, young people may take food and hoard it. This may be because they are not used to the freedom of helping themselves, they are not used to having excess food or even sufficient food around, or purely to see the reaction of the carer. Talking over the situation is certainly the best tool here.

Being 'grounded' (kept at home) for a specific time is probably the punishment young people hate the most so it is usually the most effective. Alternatively, they could be given chores to carry out or sent to another room but these should be time limited.

Young people are often led on by other young people without realising the consequences of their action. They might shoplift or play truant, thinking it's 'no big deal'. Parents, carers, teachers, social workers, and the police may all be involved. Together you could possibly draw up a form of contract agreeing acceptable behaviour and stating what will happen if the contract is broken. Another way to encourage positive behaviour is for the young person to be set agreed goals, simple, easy-to-achieve ones at first. This can be linked into a behaviour plan the school sets up for the young person.

Dealing with angry or aggressive behaviour

If the young person is very angry or aggressive then:
- Don't have a slanging match, don't swear or shout.
- Think about what you say and don't stand in an aggressive way.
- Let them be angry. Channel that anger. Let them hit their pillow or whack the mattress. You could even give them a rolled up newspaper to do it!
- If they really are aggressive, try to move them to another room for their own safety.

- **Stay calm at all costs** – if you lose your temper, you may also frighten the young person.
- When the young person has calmed down, wait for the right moment to talk to them.
- **Let them know you care.**

Later, carry out an ABC analysis (page 97). It may be something you could do together

Restraint

Restraint should be seen as an absolute last resort. Training should have been given in restraint techniques. The social worker should be immediately informed if it is necessary to use restraint and the carer should record all details carefully. Any other appropriate procedures should also be implemented. Once the situation has died down some of the strategies mentioned above should be used to try to find out:

- What caused the escalation of the situation.
- What changes could have been made that might have prevented the need for restraint.
- What changes need to be made in the future.

Caring for yourself after behaviour difficulties

Following difficult times, the carer should develop their own coping strategies in order to relieve stress. They could contact another member of their support group to talk over the situation. Don't forget to record the incident, including the lead up to it and the aftermath as soon as possible.

Privacy and confidentiality

As young people grow up they have a wish for secrecy; a desire for privacy and confidentiality. This is a very natural part of growing up and should be respected. Many parents and carers find this difficult to cope with.

Young people being looked after often hate the thought that they are talked about or that what they think they have told someone in confidence is being passed to someone else. They also hate to think that their file can easily be read by others.

We all want our privacy to be respected and young people are no different. However there are considerations and judgements to be made for instance as to when:

- Letters addressed to them should not be opened or read.
- The telephone should be put somewhere so that confidential calls can be taken if they don't have a mobile phone.
- Friends should be able to come to visit and be seen in private.
- They should have cupboards that can be locked so they can store their own belongings safely.
- They should be allowed to self-manage an appropriate budget such as the call list and payment for their mobile phones.

Carers and parents like to see things tidy: yet young people need their own space where they can leave things as they wish knowing they won't be interfered with or examined.

Sometimes if you were to go through a young person's belongings you might find drawings, writings or pictures you wished you hadn't seen or that will shock you. Usually this is just a normal part of growing up, finding out about their sexuality or expressing their feelings and emotions. They would possibly 'rather die' than think someone had seen them.

Young people need to know under what circumstances their 'space' will be entered, for example, if it is felt the young person is at risk or to clear up the room if it is a health hazard!

Carers will also have their own personal belongings – respecting privacy should be a two-way process. Privacy and confidentiality can be a good area for discussion.

Some secrets cannot be kept – if you are worried that a young person has suffered or is likely to suffer 'significant harm', you may have to take the matter further, but the young person needs to know what you intend doing, why, and to be kept informed. Let them know that you respect their confidentiality but cannot keep their secret in the circumstances.

Self-respect, confidence and self-esteem

The teacher said:

> *You are a no-hoper. You'll leave school with nothing.*

This care-leaver is now at college.

Everyone needs to be valued, to feel special, and to feel important. By treating young people as individuals, working and caring for them you will develop their self-confidence.

By making opportunities for young people to succeed you will build up their self-esteem. No matter what difficulties a young person has had in the past, they need to know that you expect them to overcome these difficulties; that they are responsible for their own life and behaviour. Treat them with respect and gradually they will learn to respect you and others around, and also to respect themselves for what they are.

? *What other questions might help young people do this?*

On the next page is an exercise called Know Yourself. Young people might like to do this on their own, with you or in a group. It may help them to look at things with fresh eyes. If young people show you their answers, you may be surprised, indignant or hurt but at least you may know the young person a little better.

You might also use it as a talking tool.

To have self-respect and to build up confidence they have to understand and know themselves, what makes them tick, and realise that they must take responsibility for their own actions.

Know yourself checklist – the 3-pointer

3 things you are good at:

1 ....

2 ....

3 ....

3 things you are not so good at:

1 ....

2 ....

3 ....

3 ways you could improve:

1 ....

2 ....

3 ....

3 likes

In food?	In clothes?	School/college work?	Other things you like
1	1	1	1 ....
2	2	2	2 ....
3	3	3	3 ....

3 dislikes

In food?	In clothes?	School/college work?	Other things you dislike
1	1	1	1 ....
2	2	2	2 ....
3	3	3	3 ....

→

What would make you change any of these answers:

....

....

....

The 3 best points about yourself:	**The 3 worst points about yourself:**
1	1 ....
2	2 ....
3	3 ....

3 ways you could improve on your worst points:

1 ....

2 ....

3 ....

What do you dislike most about other people?

1 ....

2 ....

3 ....

If it annoys you to answer this 'stupid' questionnaire, think about why...

Values

We seem to be bombarded with all sorts of guidance to ensure that young people are helped in all sorts of ways so that they learn to become responsible caring adults. However, young people still need help to learn to make decisions in their lives.

I want to know right from wrong.   young person

They need to learn to:
- Know the difference between right and wrong.
- To accept differences and that not everyone will agree with them.
- Tell the truth.
- Keep promises.
- Respect the rights and property of others.
- Act considerately.
- Help those less fortunate and weaker than themselves.
- Take personal responsibility for their actions and self discipline.

? *What does all this mean?*

It means that you, as the carer, will need to work with them, to help them develop their own sense of values. They should also be taught to reject:
- bullying
- cheating
- deceit
- cruelty
- discrimination of any sort

Many young people complain if someone cheats on them yet a little later may cheat on others. They need to learn about standards, about what is acceptable and what is not acceptable, and to think about how others feel and not just think about themselves.

As they grow up they will become aware of issues such as:
- damage to the environment
- smoking
- divorce
- loyalty
- drinking alcohol
- blood sports
- abortion
- sexuality

All good topics for discussion.

Group discussions, individual discussions, reading newspapers and watching particular television programmes are all ways that can develop a young person's beliefs.

Of course, young people will always question why things are as they are and will test the boundaries. Boundaries need to be there so that they know where they stand, so that they have something to rebel against and so that they have something to stand them in good stead for the future.

Self harm

One of the most difficult situations carers face is when confronted with a young person who deliberately harms themself. Whether it is a one-off or a regular occurrence, it causes a whole variety of strong feelings from intense anger through to fear, anxiety and sadness. Acts of self-harm are usually caused by feelings of failure and helplessness.

? *What is self harm?*

We all harm ourselves sometimes, for example, by smoking, drinking, reckless driving, and unprotected sex or simply by not always taking good care of ourselves or our diet. However, self-harm is a deliberate act which inflicts pain or injury to one's own body.

? *How do young people harm themselves?*

- Cutting or scratching (arms, legs etc.)
- Banging or bruising
- Burning
- Hair pulling
- Scrubbing with abrasives or noxious chemicals such as bleach
- Swallowing harmful substances

? *How often does it happen?*

As self-harm is often a secretive act it is not possible to know how often it occurs. It can happen once or many times, as a daily response or periodically when a problem arises. Most people who hurt themselves do so quite superficially and carefully. It is only a minority who do so severely and need outside medical treatment for their injuries. Most people stop self-harming when they begin to feel better about themselves.

? *What is the difference between self-harm and attempted suicide?*

It is not easy to draw a distinction between self-harm and attempted suicide although it is easy to believe that one might lead to the other. Both reflect deep distress but the young person who self-harms is not wishing to kill themselves but deaden the painful feelings they are experiencing. It is an attempt to cope with these painful feelings yet stay alive.

? *Why might a young person self-harm?*

- Releasing tension and feelings that have become bottled up inside, hurting so much as to become unbearable. These feelings may stem from current difficulties in life for example stress of exams, a break up with a boy or girl friend, racial harassment, confusion about sexual identity or be a response to past painful experiences for example abuse.
- Escaping for a while from painful feelings or memories.
- Making oneself unattractive in their body so keeping others at bay.
- Gaining some control – this is particularly so for young people who have been abused and were powerless.
- Punishing themselves so atoning for feelings of being bad or guilty.
- Seeking help by demonstrating their distress.
- Comforting themselves – not just the release of tension but also having something 'unique' they can do which may also gain attention and care from others.

? *How can you help a young person who is self harming or attempts suicide?*

General help may include:
- Be prepared – although unfortunately sometimes if won't be possible.
- Be aware of information on the young person's past history of self-harm or significant events that might cause distress.

- Reduce their feelings of powerlessness by consulting and acting on their views.
- Don't let their behaviour or the way you deal with it make you lose sight of the young person themselves.
- Give praise.
- Value them.
- Provide opportunities for them to talk.
- Show in your daily life that there are other ways of coping with stress and problems.
- Talk with them not at them.
- Actively listen.
- Reduce the need for self-harm and the harm itself by offering other options but recognise it may take considerable time and support.
- Encourage and create opportunities to talk, doing so at the young person's pace, in their time and place.
- Encourage other ways of communicating and expressing feelings, for example, through writing letters, keeping a diary, drawing, composing poetry, all of which need not be shared, or you could provide a punchbag or a cushion for them to hit.
- Think who else they might feel comfortable talking to.
- Be sympathetic and understanding to the feelings of shame, guilt and confusion the young person may be feeling.
- Provide practical care and comfort – a favourite meal, a pet, a bath.
- Provide basic assistance, for example, a first aid box and simple instructions to the young person – help them to help themselves – it isn't necessarily helpful to step in and do it for them.

Let them feel:
- They are being taken seriously.
- They are supported and that things will be alright again.
- A sense of perspective.
- Loved and attached to people who are hurt by their behaviour.

A carer should **not** think:
- They can stop the young person if the young person doesn't want to.
- They are responsible for the action.
- They should make the young person feel guilty.
- Of telling anyone without the young person's consent.

Remember, with help and support things can, and usually do, get better and young people find other ways of sorting out their problems and dealing with their feelings.

Listening and being listened to

A good communicator should not lie or build up false hopes. They should be trustworthy; reliable and honest and most especially, a good listener.

You cannot listen to young people all the time but you can often spot those who have something important to say by a change of behaviour or mood.

Some simple listening rules

1. Never be too busy to listen. Young people have important things to say at the most inconvenient time of the day.
2. Listen to what is being said. Give the young person your entire attention.
3. Don't anticipate what will be said next. Wait and listen. That way you'll be sure.
4. Don't judge or let your mind jump away from the topic.
5. Pay attention to both what is being said and how it is being said.
6. If you have a question, make a mental note of it and ask it at the proper time. Don't interrupt or write while the young person is talking. Asking questions can certainly help but they require careful handling and good timing.
7. If you disagree, don't get angry. Wait until they are finished. They may say something that makes your anger unnecessary or even embarrassing.
8. If the young person goes on for a long time, jot down a few notes as soon as you can. This will help later on in remembering what was said.

> **Listening is as much an art as speaking.**
> **Both require practice.**
> **Both require attention.**

A good listener will usually be listened to because they will have taken care to listen and will have thought about what they want to say.

If you specifically want to talk to a young person:

- Plan the time and place to suit both of you and if possible, tell them in advance. Don't choose a time when their favourite TV programme is on!
- Plan what you want to say.
- Jot down the main points you want to say.
- Have a pen and paper ready to make notes.
- Tell them at the start what you want to discuss.
- End by saying what is agreed and what action is to be taken.
- Don't gossip or pass on what you have heard.
- Show you are listening by your eye contact, nodding or use of body language.
- Respect confidentiality and privacy unless you feel the young person is at risk of significant harm.

If you feel you must pass on something you have been told: tell the young person concerned, explaining:

- The reasons why you are doing this.
- What you will do.
- How you will do it.
- Why you are taking that particular course of action.
- When you will be doing so.

At all times help keep them informed of what is happening. Be honest and never make promises you can't keep.

Friendships

I'm 17 going on 40...

What Steve went on to explain was that what he had been through in his life up to the age of 17 was probably as much as many people go through up to the age of 40.

I have nothing in common with anyone who has not been in care.   Young person

Again, what he was saying was that he felt that most 17-year-olds had very little else to think about other than clothes, parties and discos whereas he had to think about rent, bills, food, budgeting etc. as well.

Young people who are looked after may also have come from difficult backgrounds where they have moved around a lot and not had a chance to make 'best friends'. They may not, therefore, have gone through the usual process of making and keeping friends.

They may also be very lonely so if someone comes along and gives them some attention they may fall madly in love with them, sometimes to the exclusion of everyone and everything else. This person may also be much older than they are; a mother or father figure; car owner; someone who seems to have plenty of money. Young people who are being looked after may not have had a loving caring relationship with an adult so may be vulnerable to exploitation and grooming – see page 116. Carers should help young people become more self-aware and resilient so they do not fall prey to those who may further abuse them or where they may repeat previous negative experiences.

If a teenager has been sexually abused, their sexual awareness may be heightened or the reverse – they may be scared of getting into serious relationships or of repeating unhealthy relationships. This and other life experiences often make it more difficult for young people who have been abused to make or trust new friends.

Carers must also come to terms with their own feelings, beliefs and uncertainties before they will be able to openly discuss such matters including sex, sexuality and relationships with young people. They may also need assistance and training from their fostering agency to help them to fully support and advise a young person. The young person will need help to understand how not to repeat negative relationships and to develop their own self worth. If they feel they are worthless they are likely to seek out like-minded people, to repeat negative relationships and not strive for better.

Making and keeping friends

Some people find making friends easy: others find it very hard. Some people call someone they have just met 'a friend': others use the term with more care. A friend is someone you can trust, who you can talk to and want to spend time with.

? *How can I make new friends?*

Young people can be encouraged to have a wide variety of interests so that they can meet all sorts of other people. Young people from different ethnic and cultural backgrounds, or children with special needs may need extra help to enable them to establish links to other people and communities.

As a carer, you can:
- Help young people to build up their self respect and confidence.
- Help young people to understand themselves better, realising that not only is there probably a good reason why they behave in a certain way but also why other people behave the way they do.

One of the hardest lessons to learn is self control – not to lose their temper, to count to 10, to try to look at things from others' points of view, not just their own. The best way to learn is by example.

If a relationship is worth having then it's worth maintaining. Young people will need to learn to negotiate, compromise, make allowances and even to swallow their pride and say sorry (this goes for adults as well as young people).

Remember that, if in your home, young people are used to discussing and talking about all sorts of things and listening to others' points of view this will help them with their friendships. Some big problems encountered by young people in care are:
- Moving from a family into group living.
- Moving from group living into:
  - living in a family.
  - living on their own.
  - living with chosen friends.

If they move into a children's home or to another foster home, they often give up their friends and are only friendly with those around them. This can cause problems when they move on.
- Encourage them to keep their existing friends and also to make new friends outside the home.
- If it is possible, encourage them to stay at their friend's house and to go on school/college trips which entail overnight stays – see *Staying with friends* on the next page. This will help them to develop friendships and is also an important part of socialisation and growing up.

A new resident in a children's home may find it difficult to cope with the lack of personal attention, the noise, people constantly being around. On the other hand, children's home residents may find the move back home or into foster care difficult to cope with and the closeness hard to handle. Both groups will need help with this change.

The loneliness of living independently is also very hard to cope with for a young person who is used to having people around them all the time and someone to call on in time of need. Make sure they know of all the different points of contact available to help them, but most significantly they should know that they can come back to you and your family.

Staying with friends

Looked after young people may feel that there are a lot of rules and regulations which draw attention to the fact that their circumstances are different from others around them. For example it may take a long time before permission is obtained for the young person to go on a trip or on holiday with their carers. It is now being made clear that young people should not be disadvantaged because they are in care and their carers should be given delegated authority to make such decisions and give the necessary permissions. Guidance on a young person being allowed to stay overnight is now very much part of the law. Sleepovers are important and help the young person to develop friendships and in their general social development . Therefore:

- It should be encouraged unless there is a risk to the young person or others.
- Foster carers should be able to make these arrangements *for and with* the young person by taking the kind of care they would do for their own children.

❓ *Can I go to stay with friends?*

Yes, of course you can but your carer will need to know where you are going and who you are going to stay with just as they would for their own children.

❓ *Why do you have to do this?*

It is necessary as with any young person that your carer makes sure that you will be safe and well at all times and that there won't be any problems. Although asking questions about this may be annoying or embarrassing, it has to be done for your safety. It also ensures that there won't be people present who it would not be safe to see and that others in the household will not be put at risk.

A true story

The local police officer was saying that there had been a big party in one of the neighbouring houses where the parents had gone away on holiday. There had been lots of problems which the police had to resolve. Apparently, all the young people had told their parents, carers or guardians that they were having a sleepover with a particular friend. The parents accepted this. In fact all the young people went to the party. The police now recommend that parents, carers or guardians check by telephoning the relevant family before allowing anyone to sleepover.

Personal relationships and sex

Sex is a normal and healthy part of our lives. As a young person grows up, it is important that they discuss with someone they trust, issues about personal relationships and sex. It cannot be assumed that they have all the necessary facts they need since many looked after young people may have missed out on sex and relationships education. It may also be that because of their family circumstances they will not have been told about such matters at home or have a very confused and distorted idea. It is therefore essential that carers give help and guidance, otherwise a young person's only knowledge may have been gained from the playground or from negative experiences in their early lives. Sex is also discussed in the Health section and in the Spiritual section.

? *What is happening to my body?*

Most young people learn the basic 'facts of life' when they are quite young, say 7 or 8. This is usually a very simple explanation given at school. As they reach puberty, young people need to know about periods, wet dreams, and childbirth as well as about the many physical and emotional changes that occur. Young people in their early teens will have heard all sorts of tales. They may also pretend they know a lot more about sex than they actually do.

Sex is not just about being involved in sexual activities. It has physical, mental, emotional, individual, social, cultural, religious and political dimensions. The following chart may be helpful in giving some starting points for discussion. This chart is from *Sexuality, Young People and Care* (Bremner and Hill, 1994, Russell House Publishing) which is now out of print. However, the chart can be used by young people to help them think through different aspects of sex and sexuality. It can also be used by carers as a talking tool.

Sexual practice including celibacy	Sexual orientation	Sensuality	Social structures	Political dimensions	Institutional oppressions
	heterosexual lesbian gay bisexual attraction and desire	food sharing meals candlelight clothing fabrics exercise touch massage nature elements (wind, sun, water, earth, heat, cool, ice) aromas, oils intimacy sharing secrets dreams fantasy dance art music	marriage living together wedding rings conditioning gender stereotypes dress and grooming rites of passage – circumcision – bar mitzvah – retreats – first menstruation – tampons – sexual experience sex education dating going steady engagement	feminism women's groups lesbian and gay groups demonstrations celebrations mothers and toddlers groups black groups elders groups	sexism racism, heterosexism, ableism ageism class institutionalised legal system age of consent medical system mental health equal opportunity programme

Young people who have disabilities may need more help and support than most. Disabled young people may have the same urges, feelings and concerns as non-disabled young people. However, they may have a harder time in dealing with them because society often portrays disabled people as non-sexual. Very little information on sexual matters is aimed at disabled people, so it is important they have someone they trust to discuss these issues with. If you feel that you can't help, then there are specialist teams in children's services or charities and organisations that will be able to give advice, support and guidance.

Sex and the law

It is illegal for anyone (male or female) to have sexual intercourse with someone who is under 16 years of age *even if they consent to it*.

The government's guidance states that 'the experience of being cared for should include the sexual education of the young person'. As well as practical advice, this must cover the part sexuality plays in developing a sense of identity and the emotional implications of sexual relationships. The guidance also recognises that sexuality *'will be one of the most potent forces affecting any young person in the transition from childhood to adulthood'.* See the section on health.

The word 'sexuality' often means different things to different people. Many will think it is about being homosexual (gay or lesbian), heterosexual (straight) or bisexual. Others will refer to sexual orientation, sexual behaviour and sexual identity as being part of an overall sexuality. It is imperative young people understand the different terms and are confident about using them and can talk about them. They are also necessary to enable young people to make informed choices.

Foster carers and agency staff have a specific responsibility to talk to young people about issues of risk associated with sex and sexuality. Sex and sexuality may be experienced as either pleasurable, being associated with the good things in our lives, or problematic, provoking negative feelings.

❓ *Am I gay?*

Young people may have sexual feelings for someone of the same sex. This does not automatically make them gay. If they feel they are, or if they are unsure, they will need positive and non-judgmental support. There are groups and help lines offering help and support for young lesbians and gays, both nationally and locally.

If you feel you cannot help a young person regarding sexual orientation, there should be well-trained counsellors in your area who can help.

❓ *Can disabled people have sexual relationships?*

Yes. Their sexual needs should be discussed as with any other young person as part of their overall health and wellbeing. They are more likely to be vulnerable to exploitation or may need extra support from their carer to prevent them from being discriminated against.

Indecent exposure

This is where someone exposes themselves to someone else in what is considered an unacceptable fashion, in a public place, for example if a man exposes his penis or buttocks.

Rape

Rape occurs when one person forces another person to have sex without their consent. Rape is a very serious offence. Everyone has the right to say 'No'.

Even when two people are married, if the woman does not consent to have sexual intercourse, this is also an offence of rape.

Grooming

Grooming is a very subtle and manipulative way of getting children (and adults) to do things against their will. It is a way of trapping them, making them feel guilty or responsible. If the groomer may make the young person feel they have no way of getting away without getting into trouble. Although grooming is associated with paedophile behaviour, grooming can also be used to force young people, into gangs, into stealing or other such activities. The groomer can be an adult or a young person.

Given the subtle grooming methods used by abusers, young people may not understand that they are being exploited or being abused. They may think that they were acting from their own will and one of the ways a paedophile operates is to get the young person to accept that they are responsible for their actions and not the abuser. Young people who are desperately looking for love and affection will easily fall prey to such advances. Their desperation may prevent them noticing anything is wrong before it is too late.

Be alert, be watchful and be there when needed.

On-line grooming

The University of Central Lancashire's Cyberspace Research Unit has produced the following guidance to make carers aware of the grooming process used by paedophiles on line.

1. Friendship
Flattering a young person into talking in a private chatroom where they will be isolated. The young person will often be asked for a picture of themselves.

2. Forming a relationship
Asking the young person what problems they have, to create an illusion that they are good friends.

3. Risk assessment
Asking the young person about where they keep their computer and who else can see it so they can assess the risk of being detected.

4. Exclusivity
Making the young person feel they are the most important person in the world and getting the young person to believe they trust each other and can discuss anything.

5. Sex talk
Engaging the young person in sexual conversations and requesting sexual pictures of them. At this stage the paedophile will usually try to arrange a meeting with the young person.

Carers should talk to young people about the dangers of on-line grooming. They should also be aware of who a young person is 'talking' to on the web. They should be prepared to intervene if they think things are not as they should be.

Television, films and magazines often exploit sexuality in order to increase audience figures. Young people often see sex and sexuality as the only thing that matters if they are to have a successful relationship with someone. It is really important that young people learn about all aspects of sexuality and are confident to discuss things openly. Sex should be a normal and healthy part of our lives. As a young person grows up, it is important that they discuss, with someone they trust, issues about personal relationships and sex. It cannot be assumed that young people have all the necessary facts they need.

Neither residential carers nor foster carers should have a sexual relationship of any sort with someone who is in their care.

Broaching the topic of sex

Raise an issue or pose a question – use newspapers, TV, magazines. Consider what the young person's response might be and how you might engage in a useful discussion. If they will not respond, you could brightly state, 'I'd really like your opinion'.

Sometimes it is easier to pretend that someone you know has a problem. 'Someone I know has an 11 year old daughter who wears really low cut tops and mini skirts. Her mother is worried she may have a 'bad' reputation as there always appear to be older boys and men hanging around her. What do you think?'

Find time to just 'chill' with the young person on an individual basis, go for a coffee or soft drink and a chat. Ask them about their music, their friends, what makes them laugh, what makes them sad. *Listen*. The behaviour that the young person displays can give clues to what is going on for them. Young people may not have the communication skills to be able to describe all their difficult thoughts and feelings. However, they may be expressed by insulting language and out of control behaviour.

Remember to *listen* and *consider* your response. *Never* react negatively in a forceful way – this is likely to stop the conversation. It is better to 'fudge' disagreement – 'I'll have to think about that...I'm not sure...maybe'. If a young person gives an opinion, this can be gently challenged or questioned, rather than by laying down the law. If you lay down the law it may make the young person angry and cause them not to share their thoughts and feelings. The discussion could be ongoing. It could be picked up and built on. It will help young people to think, consider and possibly change beliefs that may have been with them for some time. It will help them begin to develop an open and healthy approach to the whole area of sex and relationships.

❓ *What if someone is doing something to me that I do not like?*

Young people need to know that they have the right to say NO. Some young people will need a lot of help and support to do so, especially if they have a history of being lead or dominated.

No one should force another person to have sex. Everyone's body is their own and they should not be persuaded to do something sexual they do not like, feel unready for or that makes them feel unsafe. If someone forces another person to have sex, that person is committing a serious criminal offence. If anyone tries to kiss a young person or touches them in a way that worries them, the young person should be taught to say no and tell someone they trust.

? *What should a young person think about before they have a sexual relationship?*

- Do I care for and trust this person?
- Will it be safe?
- Do I know enough about preventing myself or my partner from getting pregnant or catching an infection?
- Does he or she really care about me?
- Am I ready to take on the responsibility of a sexual relationship?
- Will having sex with this person at this time lead to anyone getting hurt?
- Can my partner and I talk openly and honestly about safer sex and birth control?
- Is there anything in my culture or religion that says sex outside marriage is wrong?
- Am I being pressurised into having sex by my boyfriend/girlfriend or friends?

? *When do I know I'm ready to have sex?*

Young people can have a lot of casual relationships. It is a part of growing up and living, but it can be extremely unsettling. That's why only having sex once a young person has a long-term, committed relationship is likely to be healthier and make them happier.

Feeling sexual and wanting to have sex is natural. Deciding to have sex means being responsible and being prepared to handle the consequences.

? *But everybody does it?*

Deciding not to have sex is a responsible choice. No one should have sex just because their friends say they do it. Many young people exaggerate about their relationships. Sex is only enjoyable when both partners feel right about it.

? *What is 'safe sex'?*

There is no such thing as 'safe sex', only *safer* sex. Apart from the risk of pregnancy, there is the possibility of contracting a sexually transmitted disease.

Limiting the risk of infection

The risk of infection through sex can be limited in a number of ways:

- **Not having sex**; if anyone thinks they, or their partner, has an infection (often you can't tell) be open and frank about it. If anyone thinks they have a sexually transmitted infection they should straight away go to their doctor or to a genitourinary medicine clinic (sometimes called a GUM clinic). The address will be in the local telephone directory or on the internet.
- **Limiting the number of partners**. The more partners a person has the greater the risk of getting an infection if having unprotected sex.
- **Using a BSI approved condom** properly to protect one another is an important part of safer sex but you must check the use-by date. It also helps prevent a girl getting pregnant. Condoms can be bought from garages, chemists, machines in toilets, in grocery stores, in fact virtually anywhere. They can be obtained free of charge from local family planning clinics. Condoms are available to men and women.
- **Passing urine and washing their sexual parts as soon as possible after sex** – this may help prevent passing on an infection, and also helps to prevent conditions such as cystitis (a urinary tract infection) and 'thrush' (a fungal infection).
- **Not having sex if they are drunk**. They may either forget to use a condom altogether or do not use it properly.

Contraception

There are many different types of contraception. When young people are given sex education they should also be told about the different forms of contraception that are available from family planning clinics, GP surgeries, sexual health clinics and youth advisory centres. There are also many leaflets which the carer might wish to keep at home in case the young person asks questions. At this time it is important that relationships and responsibilities are also discussed.

? *Can I get advice about contraception and sexual matters on my own?*

Yes, anyone can be given information about contraception and sexual matters but it should not be given to a young person in isolation. Discussions should take place on relationships, what getting pregnant means, both to the girl and to the boy, about decision making and only having sex because they want to and not because of the pressure put on them by other people.

Pregnancy

Contrary to popular rumours, a girl *can* get pregnant:
- The first time she has sex.
- Even before her first period.
- Even if she has a period at the time.
- Whatever position is used.
- Even if she only gets semen near her vagina without having full intercourse at all.

When a man and woman have sex they risk starting a baby: and a baby will totally change everyone's lives. That is why young people need to know about contraception and also about relationships.

Emergency contraception, commonly known as the morning after pill is available up to 72 hours after unprotected sex. It is available from a GP, sexual health clinic, accident and emergency sections of hospital and from some chemists (chemists will charge).

? *How do I know whether or not I am pregnant?*

If a young women has been sexually active, and then misses a period or their period is late, they will need to know if they are pregnant or not. Within days of having sex they can find out if they definitely are, by having a pregnancy test. They can go to their doctor, sexual health clinic, some youth drop-in clinics or buy a pregnancy test kit from the local chemist. Doing the test themselves may not be 100% reliable, especially if they do not follow the instructions carefully.

? *What about termination?*

If a young woman becomes pregnant and wishes to have an abortion she can contact her own doctor or the local sexual health clinic which gives confidential advice and counselling. It is very important that she seeks help as soon as possible.

On the other hand, the young woman may wish to keep the baby or to have the baby adopted. Counselling and practical help will be needed. Many local health authorities have specially trained staff to give this sort of help.

? *What if a boy gets a girl pregnant?*

The boy is equally responsible for a girl's pregnancy and has a responsibility to maintain the child until they are 18 years of age.

? *Is a young person legally responsible for the child?*

The Child Support Act 1991 says that parents have a legal responsibility to financially maintain any children they have, unless the child is adopted. This applies equally to both parents. Absentee parents can have deductions taken directly from their wages or have part of their benefits withdrawn to pay for the child's keep until that child is 18 years old.

Section 10

Coping With Crisis or Sadness and Improving Well-being

Expressing pain

We are all different and all have our different ways of coping with crisis. Some young people will wail and cry so you'll know they have a problem, others will bottle it up. Their unhappiness may show up with health problems such as:

Physical symptoms
- feeling their heart is beating quickly
- pains and tightness in their chest
- indigestion and wind
- colicky stomach pains and diarrhoea
- frequent passing of urine
- tingling feelings in the arms and legs
- muscle tension, often pain in the neck or lower part of the back
- persistent headaches
- migraine
- skin rashes
- difficulty focusing the eyes
- lack of self care and poor hygiene

Psychological symptoms
- unreasonable complaints
- withdrawal and daydreams
- missing school or college
- accident-proneness and carelessness
- poor work, cheating and evasion
- starting smoking
- drinking alcohol
- trying out drugs
- over-eating or loss of appetite
- difficulty getting to sleep and waking up tired
- feelings of tiredness and lack of concentration
- irritability

Unfortunately many of these may be just normal growing-up symptoms but if they persist then you may find the young person has a problem.

Some tips to help them cope
- Let them know you care.
- Be available.
- Be a good listener.
- Re-assure them.
- Suggest positive steps such as:
    - talking to their friend, teacher or relative.
    - taking part in a physical activity.
    - giving themselves a treat.

- Make them feel secure.
- Help them become independent.
- Help them to look at things from all sides.
- Get them to have a medical check-up. Many problems vanish when they find they've nothing physically wrong with them.
- If it's an emotional crisis, help them to cry.
- Have somewhere private so they can talk or cry without being heard or interrupted.

Worries

A friend of mine has a problem... or I know someone who...

If a young person starts a conversation like that, that 'someone' is often them. All the time that they can talk as someone else they won't get emotionally involved, they don't have to admit they have a problem and also they can go away and think about what you say without feeling under pressure. Follow up quite soon by asking 'what happened?' or 'has your friend?' You'll usually be told the truth then. If the matter is serious, get someone else to approach them if you feel you can't get any further.

We are all different and respond to people differently. Don't be upset if the young person tells their worries to someone else. Very few children are completely open with their own parents, preferring to talk to someone less closely involved with them, be it brother or sister, gran, neighbours, friend or teacher.

Something you and most of the world think is unimportant may be really distressing to a sensitive young person:
- be aware
- be concerned
- be patient
- be available
- be tolerant
- be understanding
- be honest
- be discreet

On the next page is a list of problems many teenagers said had worried them at some stage. Young people may like to go through the list and put a tick to describe how they feel about things at the moment.

They can, of course, do this questionnaire in confidence, but if they share it with you you'll get a pretty good idea how you can help. We all know that even the slightest worry can build up out of all proportion. A minor illness can be blown up to seem like a major life-threatening disease if there is no one on hand to share that worry with.

One young lad, who became aggressive and whose schoolwork was suffering, admitted that he thought he had cancer of the testicles. A quick visit to the doctor soon put his mind at rest.

Writing down their worries, both the facts, the situation as they see it and what can be done about it will often help. If they do it with you, you can share their worries and help them overcome them. If they can't talk to you, suggest other people who might help – teacher, social worker, relative, and friend.

Talking really is the best tool to relieve worries.

✎ Worries checklist

Here is a list of other teenagers' worries This is a problem for me at the moment:	Yes ✓	Sometimes ✓	No ✓
Having to go everywhere with adults.			
The neighbours are too nosy, they talk about me.			
I feel there are too many people bullying me.			
I worry about not having enough skills to earn my living.			
Thinking that nobody will fancy me.			
People my age not liking me.			
I don't know what I can do when I go to work.			
I may fail my exams.			
I feel all mixed up about life.			
I have no-one to help me with my troubles.			
I worry friends might turn against me.			
I am not as clever as I would like to be.			
Is there any point in living?			
I have too many arguments.			
Grown-ups are always complaining about me.			
I have to go to court.			
I stay off school, college or work too much.			
Teachers or tutors not minding their own business.			
My body is not well developed.			
I may get pregnant.			
I may get a girl pregnant.			
Having to be at home by a certain time.			
Wondering why people aren't nicer to me.			
Will I be able to do my job well?			
People talking about me behind my back.			
Having no privacy.			
I might be going mad.			
I'm not strong enough.			
I'm too fat.			

→

This is a problem for me at the moment:	Yes ✓	Sometimes ✓	No ✓
I don't know how to say 'No'.			
Not feeling very clean.			
Being bored at school or college.			
Not being allowed to pick my own friends.			
Being 'in care' – what do people think?			
What shall I tell them?			
I might not get a job			
Nobody seems to understand me.			
Not being trusted.			
Telling lies.			
I am not allowed to go places where I enjoy myself.			
Having to wear school uniform or out-dated clothes.			
Tough kids always picking on me.			
I need advice about which subjects to take for exams.			
Wondering if I will know when I am in love.			
Making a fool of myself in front of friends.			
Do people think I've done something wrong because I'm 'in care'?			
Thinking there won't be any jobs.			
Not good at sport.			
Being told off too much.			
Having too many headaches.			
I am not looking good.			
Not getting a chance to say what I mean.			
Having to keep secrets.			
I am not sleeping well.			
Being picked on by teachers and tutors.			
I am not able to talk to adults.			
Not being allowed to bring certain friends back.			
Having too many accidents happening to me.			
Getting the blame for things I haven't done.			
Not knowing what to say when out with people.			
No-one cares.			

Abuse

Young people who are looked after may have been abused in one form or another at some time in their life. Sadly, this may also occur while they are 'being looked after'.

Sometimes when a young person moves away from the parental home, their circumstances change or something happens to trigger bad memories; previous abuse may be revealed.

Many young people who have had disrupted lives may be extra vulnerable and susceptible to grooming, where someone is manipulated into doing something that they would not necessarily want to do.

A young person can also be groomed in other ways, for instance to join a gang or to steal.

What is abuse?

The main forms of abuse are:
- physical abuse
- sexual abuse
- neglect
- emotional abuse

Physical abuse

There are many kinds of physical abuse. It may be that young people are physically hurt or injured, given poisonous substances or drugs or imprisoned in some way.

Many young people who are physically abused have visible injuries, for example bruises in places that do not normally get bruised by accident, bruises of different ages, marks from beating, black eyes, burns, scalds, unexplained fractures and head injuries.

Physical abuse should be suspected where the explanation of the injury does not fit the facts or if the young person is reluctant to say how the injury happened or to explain where they have been and why.

Sexual abuse

Sexual abuse is where young people are exploited by others to meet their own sexual needs, and forced or encouraged to perform sexual acts against their will. This may be fondling, masturbation, oral sex, sexual intercourse, anal intercourse or exposure to pornographic material including videos and on the internet.

Common signs of sexual abuse are:
- Injuries or soreness in sexual areas or mouth.
- A wide range of emotional problems (see list on the next page).
- Inappropriate sexual behaviour – overly sexual or extreme fear of intimate contact.
- Knowledge and understanding of sexual matters beyond their age.
- Urinary tract infections.

Neglect

Neglect is a term used to describe the failure of a parent or carer to meet a young person's basic needs, such as providing food, warmth, medical care and shelter. This is often a very difficult thing to tackle in a young person as it can be difficult to immediately prove. Neglect is an extremely serious abuse and as with other forms of abuse it can strip a young person of any feeling that they have been or can be loved or valued.

Emotional abuse

Emotional abuse is where young people suffer as a result of a constant lack of affection, verbal attacks, bullying, racial and other forms of harassment, which undermine a young person's confidence and self-esteem.

The signs of abuse

Any of the following may be associated with abuse:
- Poor or deteriorating school or college work.
- Erratic attendance, at school or college.
- Reluctance to go to school or college or frequent early morning minor illnesses.
- Problems with sleeping or nightmares.
- Complaints of hunger, lack of energy and apathy.
- Possessions often 'lost', dirtied or destroyed.
- Desire to stay around adults or avoid adults, either generally or specifically.
- Reluctance to attend medicals.
- Being unhappy, withdrawn or isolated.
- Having a new tendency to stammer.
- Changes in eating habits, ranging from tummy aches, a lack of appetite, or excessive 'comfort eating' to more serious conditions, such as anorexia, or bulimia.
- Aggression.
- Constant attention seeking or over-pleasing or over-compliant behaviour.
- Indications of alcohol, drug or substance abuse.
- Attempted suicide.
- Running away from home.
- Low self-esteem.
- Poor hygiene.

Finally, unlikely excuses to explain any of the above, or refusing to give any reasons for the above should ring 'alarm bells'.

The long-term effects

Physical scars heal but many young people take longer to recover from the emotional trauma of abuse. In fact, some never recover. They may need professional help. Young people who have been sexually abused over a long period of time may have little understanding of what is appropriate sexual behaviour. In general, a young person who has been subjected to any form of abuse will need to be helped to understand what is good behaviour and what is not acceptable. They will have to learn this. This will be one of the most difficult issues carers will have to face as it will not always be clear from a young person's behaviour what they are reacting against. Carers must be aware of this and ensure that they do not place themselves in situations which could be misinterpreted whilst at the same time they should not reject the young person. If a young person is behaving in a certain way, they may be trying to unpick the negative messages they received in their childhood. If a young person is prevented from doing this unpicking in a safe environment such as a foster home or children's home, they will lose out on potential opportunities which could help to address their abuse.

Statistically, young people who have been in care are more likely to be amongst the neediest adults in our society. Unless they are helped when they are young they can go on to have children of their own and then, following in their parents' footsteps, end up exposing their children to the same negative experiences. It is important for carers to be part of a team who are trying to help break this cycle of abuse.

If a carer suspects abuse

Where carers are concerned that a young person has been abused, they should record their concern, share their concern with a senior staff member and consult their child protection procedures. In some cases they may have to speak to someone outside their own organisation.

Breaking confidentiality may be a big problem as some young people will tell you, begging you not to tell anyone else. Let the young person know that you respect their confidentiality but you cannot keep their secret in these circumstances – see *Privacy and confidentiality*.

If you have evidence that a young person is being abused then you **must** pass this on. You will have to explain this to the young person. They'll probably think they hate you at first but will be relieved when they know that something is being done. Keep them informed.

? How can carers help young people who may have been abused?

Carers can help by:
- Listening to what a young person says, how they are saying it, their body language and what they are *not* saying .
- Avoiding asking too many questions or asking for unnecessary detail.
- Being alert and observant.
- Protecting the young person.
- Trying to find out what a young person is afraid of.
- Where a young person is in danger of serious harm, carers must follow the procedures for protecting the young person.
- Telling the young person what you are going to do and what will happen next.
- Never telling lies to the young person or making promises you cannot keep.

Who are the abusers?

Most young people who have been abused are abused by those they know and could be someone they even like – older friends, parents, relatives, carers, neighbours. Often the abuser is also the most caring person in their life.

This is particularly difficult for the young person to cope with as they do not want to cause a problem to those close to them but that person may go on to abuse others. You will have to help young people to understand that what abusers do is wrong, that the young person is not to blame, but that everyone must be protected from the abuser.

? *What are a young person's rights?*

Young people are entitled to be protected from all forms of abuse. Let them know they are not alone and that you are there to protect them. Many young people will find it hard to talk about being abused they need to know that you can be trusted. Others may disclose abuse and then retract their allegations because they think it is too difficult to face up to the consequences.

Young people need to know:
- That you can be trusted.
- That you will believe them.
- That they are not to blame.
- That some 'secrets' cannot be kept.

Make sure you always discuss with the young person the difference between keeping secrets and keeping confidences – see *Confidentiality and secrets*.

? *What happens if I report abuse?*

When it is suspected a young person has been a victim of abuse, they may be asked to be interviewed at a special safe place by trained staff, one of whom may be from the police. A recording will be made of this interview, so the young person doesn't have to keep repeating their experiences. The recording may be used in evidence in court. A young person may refuse to give an interview.

The young person may be asked to have a medical but they may refuse providing they have sufficient understanding to make an informed choice.

Children and domestic violence

Thousands of young people witness domestic violence and it is thought that nine out of 10 of these are in the same or next room when this happens. Some children have been reported as showing signs of post traumatic stress as a result of this.

In recognition of the traumatic effect on young people who witness domestic violence, the law has extended the duty of care to include a young person who has 'suffered from seeing or hearing the ill-treatment of another'. This will include young people who have seen or heard a parent being beaten or consistently and aggressively shouted at.

Foster carers will need to be aware of how young people who have witnessed domestic violence behave. They may be afraid of anyone who reminds them of the violent person. Some young people will regress, for instance they may act younger than their chronological age and become fearful. All of them will need to learn to trust again.

Bullying

Many young people suffer badly because they are bullied. Young people who are bullied are entitled to be protected. They may not tell anyone in case they are thought of as 'grassers' or considered weak.

Many of the effects of abuse may apply to a young person who is being bullied so carers need to be observant. Studies show that over half of all young people say they have been bullied at some time.

? *What is bullying?*

Bullying may be said to be violence, physical or psychological, conducted by an individual or group and directed against someone who is unable to defend themselves in the situation.

Bullying includes:
- People calling you names.
- Making things up to get you into trouble.
- Hitting, pinching, biting, pushing and shoving.
- Taking things away from you.
- Damaging your belongings.
- Stealing your money.
- Taking your friends away from you.
- Spreading rumours.
- Threats and intimidation including over the internet or on a mobile phone.

? *Who are the bullies?*

Almost anyone can be a bully:
- children or young people of the same age
- teachers
- older children
- carers
- dinner ladies
- policemen
- caretakers
- parents
- swimming pool attendants

If you or your friend gets bullied, go and tell your teacher! If you are afraid of getting bullied, stay with your friends or family.

? *Who gets bullied?*

Anyone – but you are more likely to suffer bullying if you are:
- quiet or shy
- nervous
- solitary
- less aggressive
- smaller than your peers
- disabled

Young people with special needs and young people from ethnic minority groups are twice as likely to be called names as others.

Bullying can occur from a very young age but seems to increase with the age of the young person and is more damaging in secondary schools.

> *Bullying is most common around schools. There are always bullies in schools. They always hang around after school and before school starts. Sometimes people get bullied at playtimes and lunch time.*
> James Tallack

Bullying at school

The following are some other suggestions for young people who have been, or are being, bullied. Carers may like to pass these on or use them as a basis for discussion.

1. If they are worried that telling will make matters worse, let them know that you will be discreet.

2. Suggest the young person gets help, and talks to someone they can trust such as their social worker, teacher or someone else at school or get them to agree that you will do this for them.

3. Liaise with the school to see what action they are taking or if there has been a change in the behaviour of the young person.

If it doesn't get sorted straight away, tell them not to give up. Schools must have an 'anti-bullying' policy, they need to know what is going on and they must be active in trying to combat bullying. At the end of this section is a questionnaire that Baring Primary School in South London got their young people to complete. It may be something you could use too.

? *What else can I do?*

Tips for young people being bullied:

1. Don't let bullies think they are scaring you. Try to ignore or laugh at what they say – it's hard but worth a go.

2. If you do get angry don't let it show. Walk away as soon as you can.

3. Stay with a crowd – bullies usually pick on you when you're on your own.

4. Keep a diary. Write down what happens each time you are bullied, what is said, when and where. Give this information to those who are helping you.

5. Time your visits, for instance go to the toilet when you know you will not be on your own.

6. Take up self defence! This doesn't mean 'fighting back', but it will make you feel more confident. Ask about self defence classes where you live.

7. If you are bullied through your mobile phone or on the internet, keep a copy of the material and show it to a trusted adult who can help you deal with it.

No-one should tolerate bullying and carers need to make it clear that bullies have no place in their home.

Victim support

If the young person has been a victim of crime, there is a national telephone support service designed to help victims or their advocates. They will be able to give young people advice about what to do as well as what services are available to them locally.

The Criminal Injuries Compensation Authority (CICA)

It is possible that the young people you foster will have been a victim of crime. For the purposes of the Victim Support Service, it does not matter whether the abusers were convicted, what is important is that a crime was committed. It is essential, therefore, to be aware that a young person may be entitled to specific services or compensation under this scheme.

Those eligible will be covered if:
- Someone took or tried to take or damaged their property.
- Someone suffered physical or mental injury.
- The crime was intended or likely to injure or kill.
- A sexual offence was committed.

The authority will:
- Offer advice as to eligibility for compensation under this scheme.
- Process applications for compensation effectively and sensitively.
- Aim to reply to all correspondence within 20 days.
- Explain if compensation is refused and advise how a decision can be reviewed.

Loss and bereavement

At any age, losing someone or something you love even for a short time may be a very painful experience. Young people in care may hear about the death of someone they know and may not be alongside the person when they die so it is important carers are prepared and able to help when the situation arises.

More significantly, young people in care are likely to have suffered more losses than other children:
- their family
- their home
- their room
- their siblings
- their pets
- their school
- in fact anything

Many of these losses will leave a young person with the same feelings they would have if they had had a suffered the death of an important person.

Many young people will have the same types of questions about death:
- What does it mean?
- What causes it?
- What happens afterwards?
- Why did it happen?

Carers need to be open about the issue of death and can, for instance, talk about the ageing changes that occur throughout life, how illnesses cause different changes and why people die. It may be that a young person experienced death at a younger age but now wishes to discuss the matter more fully. This is normal and would usually indicate that the young person is ready to find out more about their loss and can understand more fully or feel more secure about the matter.

The young person may have regrets about not saying goodbye, about not attending the funeral, about things they said to the person or even about the thoughts and feelings that they had for them. Carers could talk about the feelings and emotions of the different people involved: how different people will react in different ways and how it is common to feel the range of feelings between intensely missing them to being very angry with them.

When a death occurs, carers may also need to remind the young person what the words mean and explain, probably more than once, what is happening. Rituals around death vary depending on culture, beliefs or religion. The carer may have to get more information so they can help and support the young person specifically with rituals that are being organised. They will need help to understand and accept their situation. The power of symbolism can be very important in some situations as in the example below:

> *I spent the day of the funeral in a state of limbo, not able to settle or knowing what to do as I was not going to the service. Eventually, my husband suggested that I should buy a rose bush to plant in our garden in memory of my father. We bought a bush and chose 'Peace' rose which had been my mother's favourite when she was alive. The amazing thing was that once we had planted the rose I felt totally calm and at peace with myself.*

Although such symbolism may not be possible for a young person what will be helpful is finding a way of demonstrating, acknowledging and remembering the death and life of the person. For instance:
- Visiting a place of worship together.
- Having your own memorial service.
- Going to a favourite place.
- Making and eating a favourite dish.
- Launching a balloon with a note attached to it.
- Having a party or get together to celebrate the life.

On hearing the news of the loss of someone they know and love they will experience many feelings, such as a sense of shock and disbelief, a numbness.
This may be followed by:
- misery
- anger
- questioning
- sadness
- self-blame
- blaming others

If a young person knows in advance that the loss is going to occur they will have time to prepare themselves mentally. The impact of the loss is much greater if the loss is sudden. Different young people react to death in different ways. They may:
- Cry.
- Go for long walks alone.
- Hide in a crowd.
- Be angry.
- Eat too much or too little.
- Smoke or drink alcohol to excess.

Let them find their own way. When the time is right, talk to them or let them talk to you. In today's diverse society explanations about death are many and varied, so you may need to seek specialist advice. It is something you might do with the young person.

? *How does talking help?*
- It can dispel wrong ideas.
- It helps to make sense of the loss.
- It helps to lift the burden of responsibility that many young people will feel. For example if there was a car crash and they survived and their mother didn't, they may feel guilt. If they were out enjoying themselves at a party when their father died they may say 'if only...'

Sometimes this burden may be realistic and they will need help to come to terms with this. If the person who has died was the abuser, memories may come flooding back. There may be renewed questioning, re-awakening of feeling, unsettled emotions and much of the previous work with the abused young person may need to be repeated.

? *How long will it take to get over it?*

Young people will feel pain, let them. Don't try to get them to get over it too quickly. There is no set time that grieving lasts but some people believe that the process of loss can take as long as five to seven years.

They will feel desolation and despair. They may feel there is no light, no purpose, and no point in their lives.

Who am I?   What does it mean for me?   I'm an orphan.

…may be said many times.

The pain will recur again and again – at birthdays and anniversaries, at Christmas and holiday times and at other times that were special for the particular family. There are times in their life when the loss may be re-experienced such as weddings, the birth of their own child, leaving school.

Life moves on and the young person will adapt and adjust but bereavement is never fully dealt with but can be managed and accepted so long as the young person has been allowed and encouraged to grieve.

Help them find practical things they can do, such as collecting mementos or photographs or writing down how they feel.

Leisure: what to do in your free time

Young people will find life more fun if they have interests outside the home. It will:
- Help them build self-confidence.
- Give them a purpose, something to aim for, to achieve.
- Help them make new friends.
- Give them somewhere different to go. This is especially important when they 'leave care'.

Many young people will need a lot of help and encouragement to begin with.

Sport
? *I like sport, what can I do?*

Most towns have public amenities such as swimming pools, skating rinks, sports and leisure centres, tennis courts and football pitches. The young person could use any of these by themselves or with friends or they could join a sports team.

There are sports that disabled young people can take part in, such as wheelchair basketball, rugby, hockey or tennis. Many areas offer cheaper prices for young people.

Music

? *I like music, what can I do?*

They could:

- Learn to play a musical instrument.
- Form or join a band.
- Make a recording.
- Go to gigs or concerts.

Art

? *I like 'arty' things; what can I do?*

They could:

- Paint, draw, act, or just watch.
- Join clubs for photography, stamp collecting etc.
- Go to art galleries or museums.
- Look for leaflets in their local library about classes, exhibitions or clubs, or go to their local arts centre and talk to the people there.

Clubs

? *Can I join a club?*

There are a variety of youth clubs offering many different activities for young people. There are also uniformed groups such as guides and scouts. They are a good way of making new friends and none of them cost very much to join or to attend. There may also be youth clubs specifically for young people with special needs though some young people will prefer to attend a youth club for everyone. Let them choose.

The young person may feel too shy to join a club. Why not ask a friend to go with them? Tell them it can be fun when they start something new – and it will give them something to talk about with their friends, or with adults, or at a job or college interview.

What else is there to do?

- Young people may like to attend a church, mosque or synagogue for example. They will meet many new people and make new friends.
- There are countryside and environmental projects to take part in or visit.
- It is worth visiting village halls, community schools and community centres to find out what is going on there.
- Go rock climbing, scrambling, abseiling, mountain bike riding or go on adventure holidays.
- If they don't want to go to a club or take part in sport, there are plenty of other things they can do, such as reading, making their own clothes, cooking or woodworking. Try getting them to learn a new skill.
- They could also become a volunteer in anything from helping old people to protecting the environment. Get them to think of something that really interests them and then find out how they can go about helping.

To find out more there will be leaflets at:

- local libraries
- local arts centres
- sports or leisure centres
- education offices
- youth and community service offices
- National Youth Agency
- on the internet

Doing something in your spare time can help when you apply for a job.

For example if they were a member of a netball team or football team it could show that they:
- Are reliable – turning up for each match.
- Are punctual.
- Can follow the rules.
- Get on well with others.
- Can work as part of a team.
- Have leadership qualities.
- Have self-discipline.
- Can make a regular commitment.

Do they know where the information on leisure activities is kept in your home or how you or they can find out on the internet? Is there a file for everyone to use?

I don't want to do anything!
It requires considerable confidence to try something new. Remember those fears 'Will I make a fool of myself?' Some young people may have had their self-esteem so battered by their experiences that they may want to stay in bed all day or mope around. Your motivation skills may be sorely tried before a young person takes up a new interest. An invitation to come and see rather than come and sign up is often the best approach.

However, adolescence is a time when many teenagers withdraw and want to be by themselves. If the young person is like this it may be necessary to help them through this period before they can be more involved with other activities.

The electronic age: TV, computer games, surfing the net and smart phones

There is a great deal of debate about the pros and cons of young people watching TV, playing computer games and using the Internet. These technologies are here to stay so we need to help young people to use them wisely. Carers will also need to understand the range of things that can be done on a smart phone.

What is known is that:
- If a young person has a tendency to have epileptic fits then TV or computer screens may start them off because of what is known as 'flicker fusion'.
- Some young people will tell you that some computer games make them feel frustrated and even violent.
- Watching violence on TV may also give a young person violent feelings or desires to experiment.
- Watching TV, playing computer games or surfing the net means a young person is inactive, is not talking to other people, is not getting fresh air, playing with others, or getting exercise.
- A young person may have difficulty discerning fact from fiction.
- Some TV programmes billed for young people are totally unsuitable in their use of language and presentation.
- You may not be able to control how a young person uses their smart phone.
- A young person may be contacted on their mobile phone by people who may be harmful to them.

Computer games can help a young person with their school work; will certainly help their hand-eye co-ordination and can give many young people a great deal of pleasure.

Watching TV can also be pleasurable as well as teaching young people about current affairs, wildlife and nature and many other interesting topics. It can also fill a need for lonely young people as they come to regard the presenters as their friends.

Using their smart phone, young people can download many apps to help with their education and leisure time.

A true story

Aysha was a Muslim aged 15. She had two sisters, one slightly older and one a little younger. They were all bought up in a very traditional fashion. Her teacher was amazed when she overheard Aysha talking about the most explicit sordid and sexual events. It transpired that she and her sisters hired pornographic videos from the local shop, taking them home in different covers and watching them in their room – a case of no-one checking on what the young people were watching.

What carers can do
- Discuss very carefully the TV programmes and games the young person should watch or play and help the young person to learn to choose selectively.
- Sit with them and discuss what has happened, what you both have seen and what you think and feel about it.
- Agree on the amount of time in a day a young person may sit in front of a screen and encourage them to take part in other more physical and personally interactive activities as suggested above.
- Manage the use of the Internet and, if possible, their mobile.
- Screen the computer games or Internet a young person has access to. Some people are not always careful and leave unsuitable material lying around or available.
- Show an interest in the computer games, use them with the young person and talk about them. In this way unsuitable material should not be brought into your home.
- Be aware that the young person may be under pressure from their peers to play particular computer games or watch particular TV programmes or be continually on social networking sites.
- Talk with parents about which TV programmes the young person watches if this is appropriate.

It has also been discovered that in addition to young people being addicted to computer games, there is now an accepted psychological disorder called Internet Addiction Disorder (IAD) for people who cannot stop surfing the net.

Some Internet providers offer control systems as part of their monthly packages. It is also possible to buy programmes which cut out upsetting or inappropriate activities. Make sure your system has an appropriate control installed. You may also consider restricting the young person's use of their mobile (see next page).

Many young people access Internet chat rooms. This is fraught with dangers. Paedophiles are known to pose as a young person in order to make contact with them.

Never let a young person meet someone from a chat line unaccompanied.

Never let them give out any personal information over the Internet.

Always warn, and remind them, of the dangers.

Mobile phones

The better the phone the more likely it is to be stolen.

Mobile phones are not just used for talking, texting and sending e-mails. Smart phones are more sophisticated and offer better and quicker Internet services. For example if a photo is taken using the phone it can immediately be downloaded onto Facebook for everyone to see.

Mobile phones have parental controls. These let you do things such as:
- Block selected websites and email addresses by adding them to a filter list.
- Set time limits for use.
- Prevent young people from searching certain words.

Before you set rules you can check the equipment's user manual or contact the mobile phone operator to find out about any young people safety measures they offer. The rules for use should, however, be discussed and worked out with the young person.

Children and young people should understand that they should never be afraid to tell you about frightening or bullying emails or messages they get with unacceptable content. It's not their fault that they have received them and the addresses can be added to the parental control filter list.

Working out which contract or pay-as-you-go service to use is a personal matter but is a good exercise to do together.

A young person should not have a phone with a camera until they can prove they are able to use the camera responsibly (see James' story on the next page).

Many phone operators offer a location service which tells allocated people where the person is. It is a way of helping to keep a young person safe but can cause problems as they think you do not trust them.

Schools usually ban mobile phones from their premises and this rule should be followed, though some young people will try to take their phones with them.

There is a text language which has developed that young people use. Sometimes it is indecipherable to adults. Using this text language all the time can affect school work and pieces of work have been handed in where text language has been used by young people, often without realising.

If a young person is being mugged or bullied into handing over their phone, they should just hand it over. Their well-being is far more valuable than a phone.

There should be an agreed procedure, worked out with the young person, to inform someone if they feel they are being bullied via the phone, from a text, e-mail or an actual call. Mobile phone numbers should only be given out to friends and family.

A true story

When James was experiencing normal sexual desires he would photograph his penis and send a photo to his friends. Unfortunately, on one occasion he sent it, by mistake, to a 14 year old girl who was very upset.

A true story

Joe was 15 and had his first girl friend, Labamba. She lived about 10 minutes walk away from Joe's house. However, when not at school they seemed to spend all their time on their mobile phones. On one occasion, Chris, his father, asked Joe if he was sure that he hadn't used more than his allocated free texts and calls. 'No', was the answer but when his dad checked Joe had over-spent by more than £500 which he is still paying back! Chris contacted the operator to complain that some warning should have been given but was told it was the user's responsibility.

Social networking sites

> **If you don't want people to know something, then don't put it on line**

A young person's guide to social media

You have the power to build something really incredible. Just do it but remember:

- Everything you type can be searched and used for or against you. Your digital footprint is permanent. What you say is who you are.
- Reveal. Everybody is watching, maybe not right now, but they will be. Will they see the person you want them to see?
- Respect. Only type what you would say to that person's face because they will see it and show it to other people. Or, their mum might call. Or, their friends will come after you. Or...
- Who you hang out with online reflects on who you are in real life. Join up, hang out or start with people who share your values. Follow people you like and respect.

Decide, together, how much you monitor the young person's activity online. The most vigilant carers will have installed online monitoring software that records everything typed and everywhere visited. However, it comes down to trust.

Think about – Do you trust them? Will they trust you if you secretly monitor them and then report on your findings? How concerned are you about their safety? Who would you share your own online records with?

Sometimes a young person gets angry when the person closest to them does this checking. Another family member or close friend may be willing to help. Decide together how often the sites should be checked: sit with them when you are doing it to decide what should be removed and who should no longer be a 'friend'. Some young people may be particularly prone to becoming involved with inappropriate people on site as they may be lonely or want to have lots of friends. They may also misinterpret signals from others.

It is important to talk with the young person about what is and is not okay to share online, especially when it comes to sensitive or private information.

Set up times to talk about what's happening on the social networking site. What's cracking them up? What's interesting? What groups do they belong to and why? What's going on with their friends?

A point of warning – many companies check the Twitter and Facebook sites of people applying for jobs. If they do not like what they see the person will not get an interview, let alone a job.

A true story

Sam was twelve. He was friendly with two girls who were his neighbours. They were a little older than Sam. On one occasion, Natasha, the younger girl, posted several very inappropriate and unkind comments about Sam on Facebook. She asked others to comment. Unfortunately, for Natasha, but good for Sam, the questions somehow also went to Sam's gran who immediately contacted Natasha's parents and had the questions removed. Natasha had not realised how many people received her Facebook comments and was much more careful in future about what she posted on the site. Fortunately, Sam knew nothing of the event.

Section 11
Money

Money matters!

The way allowances work does not help young people to get a sense of reality   carer

If you don't ask you don't get it.   young person

It ought to be written down the money you're entitled to.   young person

I share with the young people how much money we have. I think the reality that there is only so much money available is useful for them to know.   foster carer

Young people and carers agree that:
- Learning to manage money is an important skill.
- Knowing what is available and how it is shared out is important – it gives them a sense of reality.
- Young people should be told what everyone is entitled to and why. It will help them understand why some young people seem to get more than others.
- Young people need to know so they can make choices in their day-to-day lives.
- Young people should be involved in decision making on how the money is spent so they can learn how to budget and plan for their future.

What young people are entitled to

Some local authorities give clear guidelines on how money should be allocated and spent. Others leave it to the discretion of foster carers, home managers, social workers and even area managers. Whatever the system, young people need to be told about what they will get both now and in the future and they need to be involved in deciding how any special allowances are spent. They may also need your help to get it!

A true story

A young man from Birmingham was very upset because his carer had decided, without consultation with him, that a particular allowance should be spent on an iPod and download of his native language, Punjabi. He desperately wanted a pair of special trainers similar to those worn by the rest of his basketball team. He gave up playing in the team because he was too embarrassed to wear his own trainers. He flatly refused to listen to the tapes. He was very angry and resentful.

The carer, with the best will in the world was giving 'due consideration to the young person's religious persuasion, racial origin, cultural and linguistic background' but not considering the rights and responsibilities of that young person as an individual. The carer also made the fundamental mistake of not speaking with the young person and offering him a choice.

This is a difficult area but if money matters are discussed freely then young people will know what to expect and when. Special circumstances for giving extra money should be kept to a minimum.

> *I would give the girls a certain amount each month and call it health money*
> *so they can buy their own toiletries etc.*
>
> carer

Local authorities are required to provide money for young people who wish to further their education and for those young people 'leaving care':
- Find out exactly what money is available.
- Work hard to make sure they get it.
- Make sure young people are treated fairly.
- Make sure young people know well in advance what they can expect.

They'll thank you for it! Money matters must be seen to be fair.

Any young person who is employed should be expected to contribute towards their maintenance, pay for their own clothing and their personal expenses. If their wages are insufficient to meet all these costs, the local authority should ensure that the foster carer is not receiving less maintenance, nor the young person receiving less than their peers. This also applies to young people who are in full time education who may receive additional allowances.

The following is a simple suggested formula to work out a weekly contribution if a young person gets a job:
- Agree with the young person what the take home pay is – excluding overtime payments, bonuses etc.
- Deduct weekly fares and lunch allowance.
- One quarter of the remainder is what the young person should contribute to their upkeep.

> *They need to be encouraged to save because when they leave care the money*
> *will have to cover bills, rent, food as well as having a good time.*
>
> carer

Managing money

> *My friends think I'm better off being 'in care'.*
>
> young person

...and, of course, they may be right from a material point of view. It would seem to an outsider that there is an allowance for everything – a new bike, for outings, school trips, for hobbies and clothes. Learning how to manage money is important to everyone. Young people will need special help in this area as their circumstances may never be quite the same again. Keeping a budget plan is a good idea to help them manage their money. On page 145 is one they might like to use.

? *What do I need to think about?*
- What they need each week.
- Where the money will come from.
- Whether it will cover their expenses.
- If it won't, what they can do about it.

Young people also need to learn about the reasons and importance of saving money and the different methods available to them.

Bank accounts and savings

Many young people (and adults too) like to have cash because it is easier to use. However, it is also easier to spend, which may often mean wasting money. Cash can also get stolen or lost. It is a good idea to encourage the young person to open a bank account and to only draw out so much money at a time.

Young people need to understand the difference between a credit card and a debit card and how important it is to keep good records of what they have used them on and to ensure they make regular payments to pay them off.

Banks and building societies are keen to give advice and help. Research shows that once a person joins a particular organisation they very often stay with that bank or building society throughout their life. These companies offer a variety of inducements to get a young person to join and it may be you could work out together which one offers the best value for money.

To open an account a young person will need:
- Some form of identification such as passport, ID card or driving licence.
- Letter of introduction from an adult.
- Letter of introduction from a school or college.
- A small amount of money.

They will usually need to go along to meet someone from the bank or building society. Before this they should have obtained and gone through the leaflets from the different banks to see which one suits them best.

Avoiding debt

Even the cleverest person sometimes gets in a muddle with money, so it's important that young people understand how difficult budgeting is and that they get plenty of practice before becoming independent. Everyone's needs are different, so is what is important to them. Here are a few ideas on how you could help young people to save on outgoings: The list is based on one produced in Stepping Out by the Fostering Network.

? *How can I cut down on my expenses?*
- Buy clothes that last and won't go out of fashion too quickly.
- Buy clothes at sale time.
- Don't buy clothes which are 'dry clean only' – they are expensive to clean.
- Walk, if possible, rather than use bus, car or train – it's healthier and saves money.
- Use a bike – buy a second-hand one but make sure is it roadworthy before you use it. Ensure you actually know how to ride it properly. Cycle proficiency tests are well worth taking.
- Use the library for books.

- Avoid late-night corner shops, because, although they tend to be convenient, they are expensive.
- Buy groceries etc. in bulk with friends. If they're becoming independent soon perhaps it's something a group could do together.
- Cook for friends – take it in turns – it's cheaper than eating out and can be fun.
- Get a season ticket if you travel regularly.
- Car boot sales, jumble sales, markets and auctions can provide good cheap finds, whether it's clothing, furniture, books or other household goods.
- Get a free haircut by being a model on a training night at the local hairdressers' training school.
- Keep heating bills down by making sure there are draft excluders around doors and windows. Also turn off the heating when you are out.
- Wear more clothes rather than turning up the heating.
- Ready-cooked and take-away food can be expensive, so try cooking more meals from scratch.
- Fresh vegetables are cheap to buy and very nourishing.
- Buying meat from a local butcher is often cheaper than supermarkets and they usually sell cheaper cuts as well.
- Avoid buying goods on credit or hire purchase (also known as HP).
- Giving up or reducing smoking is not just good for health but it is an excellent way of saving money!

? *What about debt?*

- Should a young person get into debt, they will also need to know where they can go for help and advice.
- Is there a debt counsellor in your area?
- Is there someone from children's services who could help?

✎ Managing money, budgeting and saving checklist

Fill in these charts to work out where your money is going.

Outgoings	Weekly	Monthly	Annually
Rent			
Food			
Travel			
Clothes			
TV Licence and/or rental			
Council tax			
Water rates			
Electricity			
Gas			
Laundry			
Cleaning materials			
Soap, make-up, deodorant etc.			
Drink			
Cigarettes			
Presents			
Entertainment			
Credit/HP/loans			
Other			
Total			

Income	Weekly	Monthly	Annually
Take-home pay			
Benefits			
Housing benefits			
Other			
Total			

Income			
Outgoings			
What's left?			

Notes

Section 12

Becoming Independent

This section has been written for care-leavers to help them prepare for the next stage of their life. However, some young people have different needs that must be addressed when moving on from foster care. If you are caring for young people who fall in the categories below you should ask for more information on the support and services available for them:

- young people with disabilities
- young parents
- unaccompanied asylum seeking children
- young people placed out of their home authority

After care: a young person's view

Today's care leavers are tomorrow's citizens and parents. Moving into adult life from public care is an important transition so the success or not of that process will have a major influence on how a care leaver manages in adult life. The views and experiences of those who have already made the journey into adulthood are central to the thinking and planning that needs to take place. An 18-year-old who had recently left care was asked what she thought should be provided for care leavers. Although this was written some time ago many young people are still not getting the help and support they need to cope with the demands of adult life. This list, therefore, still applies.

The following is exactly what she wrote down in no particular order, just as it came to her:

- There should be hostels and flats with a live-in warden. Normal renting rules should apply: interview, deposit, contract etc. It should be available to everyone.
- There should be consistent aftercare advice and help for all.
- There should be drop-in centres for care leavers especially in an emergency.
- There should be a proper meeting with your social worker, carer, possibly parents and the young person to discuss all the arrangements before you leave care. This should include an aftercare booklet.
- There should be a full back-up system if things don't work out. This should be settled before you leave.
- Social services should check your living accommodation fully.
- Moving out should be a gradual process.
- Plans should be made so that young people who have recently left care and who have nowhere to go, have somewhere they can drop in especially at times such as Christmas.
- There needs to be a helpline for everyday matters.
- There needs to be a list of people who are willing to listen and give advice, i.e. education, careers, money, sexual, religion, culture etc.
- There should be an emergency 24-hour line for problems – drugs, suicide, sexual, family affairs.
- There should be an emergency refuge where they can get you in touch with someone to talk to or a place to stay temporarily.

It may be helpful if you and the young person work closely with the young person's own worker on how best to move towards independence.

Preparation and planning

What will happen to me when I leave care? young person

This is the most common worry young people have. They see news coverage about homeless young people and worry that it might turn out to be them. Young people need you to talk about and plan their future. You cannot start too soon. Indeed you start from the day that they come into your home. You provide a sense of family life: an opportunity for them to take risks and make mistakes but to be supported and to learn from them. Most importantly you are there for them and hopefully after they leave you will be available to offer advice and support, be a listening ear or just share good news as well as the sad or bad bits. Everyday things such as spending pocket money or contributing to planning a meal are all skills needed later in life. You should help them to gain the confidence and resilience to cope on their own. There is a checklist at the end of this section that they might like to use.

Young people will need:
- Life skills – like coping with crisis and making and keeping new friends.
- Money skills – like budgeting, saving and filling in forms.
- Practical skills – like changing a plug, cooking and cleaning.
- Information on how to keep healthy.

Remember! There is legislation which sets out a framework for preparing and supporting every care leaver underpinned by key principles including:
- The responsibility on the part of the corporate parent (often known as children's services) to ensure the move to independence is a positive one.
- The young person being fully involved in planning for their future.
- The young person being valued and enabled to maintain existing relationships.
- The support and help available if things go wrong being addressed.

Make sure you talk to the young person's social worker or leaving care worker about how to fulfil your role and responsibilities in working together with the young person and their family to make the transition a good one.

? When can I stop being looked after?
- When they are 18. However, young people should not be made to leave a placement before the age of 18 unless they feel ready to do so.
- When the young person, their carers, their social worker and those with parental responsibility think they are ready. Legally young people have a right to be supported to maintain contact with those people with whom they have established a strong ongoing relationship beyond 18 so long as there are no remaining risks.
- If the young person is on a care order, when the court decides the young person no longer needs to be looked after.
- Many local authorities are enabling young people to remain until they are 21 or 23, especially if they are still in education.

? Will I still be able to contact children services?
Yes, they must continue to give advice and help young people aged between 16 and 21 (25 if in full time education) who have been looked after. Young people should also be able to visit and see their foster carer or key worker. The best way to look at the transition to adult life is to see it as an ending of one part of your life and as a new beginning.

[?] *Do I have to move on?*

Yes, a time will come when the young person will need to take their steps into adulthood.

[?] *Will I still be able to go back to visit?*

Yes, most foster carers will welcome young people back for visits and it is hoped you will still remain part of their extended family. Some young people find moving on a really big problem and need to go back to their previous home regularly at first.

Making a plan

[?] *Will I get help to prepare for becoming independent?*

Yes. A joint plan, called a Pathway Plan, should be drawn up between the young person, the carer, their social worker, and others involved such as their school, a leaving care worker, the housing department or health authority. Good formal planning starts at 15 so together with the young person it is possible to take time to think about and prepare for the future to avoid shocks and big mistakes. It allows for young people to leave when they are ready making sure everything is in place before and after they move on.

The plan should show:
- What they are going to do when they move on (education, training and employment).
- Where they are going to live.
- What help they will receive.
- Who will help them.
- What happens if things go wrong.
- How they will manage financially.

Everyone involved should be given a copy.

You could also encourage them to join a national leaving care group of other similar young people or join or form a local group, so they can support each other.

[?] *Will I get any money to help me buy what I need?*

There is usually a 'one-off' allowance that should be given by your social worker. Most young people are entitled to this. Make sure they get what they are entitled to.

If they stay in full-time education they can receive financial support until they are 21 years old or until the completion of the course

If, after being independent, they decide to study, they may still be entitled to an allowance.

Citizens Advice Bureaux, Welfare Advice Centres and Housing Associations will normally be able to tell them of any money they might get. Most telephone numbers will be in the phone book or be available on the web. Help them to get as much money as they are entitled to.

The most important thing they will need is re-assurance. It will be a very big step for them:
- Arm them with all the facts you can.
- Help them get all their allowances.
- Let them know that someone cares.
- Tell them that there will always be someone to turn to in time of need and they are not alone.

Training

Local authorities produce young people's guides which have many useful contact numbers and information.

Many local authorities provide training courses to help young people cope with the problems of leaving care. What young people often need most is help in coping with the emotional side of things – that is where you come in!

There are also many courses to help carers prepare young people to become independent.

Housing

When a young person is ready to leave care their choice of what sort of place to get will depend largely on where they want to live.

? Where can I live?

Young people usually say they're going to get a flat or stay with friends. Both of these are often much more difficult than they realise.

Although staying with friends can be useful while they are getting themselves sorted out and costs little or no money, it may mean sleeping on the floor, having no privacy and losing their friends if they stay too long! Their friends may also lose any benefits they are entitled to as well.

Not only is renting a flat very expensive it can also be very lonely if a young person is on their own. Local authorities have a duty to help any young person who has been 'in care'. This may mean helping them find suitable accommodation. There may be someone specially appointed for this task or you and the young person can do it together.

Other choices they might think about are:
- Go back to live with family or relatives.
- Find lodgings in someone's house.
- Share a house or flat with other people.
- Find a bedsit.
- Live in a hostel.
- Find bed and breakfast accommodation but only for a short period.
- Live in supported lodgings if they are available.

? What should I think about?

Young people need to:
- Think about the good points and bad points of each.
- Make a list of what would be their ideal.
- Make another list of what they would accept.

Then you can go about helping them find a suitable place.

Accommodation checklist

A young person could go through the following checklist when they have found somewhere they think is suitable to live.

Accommodation checklist

Is it near work/college/shop/bank/buses/trains?

Cost per month? _____ which equals cost per week?	Deposit? _____ **Get it back?** Yes/No
Pay rent?	Weekly/monthly
What's included?	Rent/gas/electricity/rates/tv/phone/other
Notice to leave by you or landlord?	Weeks/months
Contract to sign?	Yes/No
Have you or someone else read it? Checked it?	Yes/No Yes/No
Rent book?	Yes/No (get it signed **every** time you pay rent)
Inventory (list of what's there) Checked correct?	Yes/No Yes/No
Does everything work and in condition stated?	Yes/No *If not, agree with the landlord who will get it repaired and how the repair is to be paid for.* Don't sign anything until this is done.
Read the meters? Agreed with landlord?	Yes/No Yes/No

Watch out for high rate meters that use money fast!

Careers

Local authorities must by law provide a careers advisory service although the title may vary across the UK. What is available will also vary from area to area. Some authorities provide an extra allowance so that young people looked after can be given extra help if they need it.

? *Must I go to their office?*

The careers centres will welcome both carers and young people and give help and advice not just on what jobs are available but also:
- opportunities in further education
- opportunities in training
- schemes for young people
- voluntary work
- career preparation and planning
- counselling and vocational guidance

In fact, they will provide all kinds of information, support and help for a young person taking the next step in life. Young people with disabilities should receive additional help if needed.

Occasionally someone from the careers service may be willing to come to work with the young people in their own environment.

Whatever the circumstances, find out what is available and try to get young people to make the best use of it.

Some young people will already have an idea of what they think they want to be, be it a hairdresser, a nurse, a footballer or a builder or whatever. They will need help to look at all the options.

Many schools and colleges offer young people the chance to take part in a work experience programme – see below. Encourage everyone to take part. It can be a good way of finding out – or making sure of – what they do, and don't want to do.

Try also to get them to think of the longer term rather than to think only of the present and of just getting any old job. The money they get initially might be good, but probably won't improve much in the future when they have other commitments.

Some young people think the government training schemes are a waste of time but it is not usually the case and it gives an opportunity to learn new skills and obtain qualifications. Discourage them from turning down this option out of hand. Try to get them to think about it first. You could also visit the scheme with the young person.

Some young people feel that to employers there is a stigma around those who are in care. Prepare them in case they come across this. Give them help and advice on how to handle the situation. Help them to have an answer ready in case they are asked 'Why?'

Work experience and internships

A work experience placement will be offered to most young people by their school when they are about 15 years old. This may last between one and two weeks.

Each young person will be asked to complete a form giving their choices of the type of work in which they are interested. As far as possible a placement will be found that closely meets the child's wishes.

Work experience is a good a way of finding out what a young person might want to do as a career. Many girls say they want to be a hairdresser yet after a week's work placement they realise it is the last job they would like to do! In other words do give them a fairly free choice of what they might do as it is a good way of finding out about themselves.

Whilst on work placement, normal employment rules apply regarding time keeping, dress and appearance and lateness.

When young people cannot find the work they would like to do it may be possible for them to volunteer for some work experience, often called an internship. Opinion is divided on this. Some say it is an excellent way of learning about a job, about proving oneself able to do the work and experiencing the workplace. Others say that companies are taking advantage of young people by either not paying them at all or by paying them an extremely small sum, often for a lot of hard work.

Getting a job

Remember: many employers now look at a person's social networking site before considering them for a job.

Helping a young person to choose a job and actually get it requires skill and patience. Although many schools and colleges give very good advice, a young person will probably listen to the person closest to them – you.

Some things to think about and some hints for getting a job.

? What kind of job do I want?

Do you want:
- To use your existing qualification, skills and knowledge?
- A manual job or an office job?
- To work on your own or with other people?
- To work indoors or outdoors?
- A job where you dress smartly or where you can wear casual clothes all the time?

Do you mind working evenings, weekends or shifts?

? How do I find the right job?
- Talk to as many different people as you can, look on the internet or seek out careers advisors, youth workers etc.
- Don't just think about one type of job but collect information about others that might suit you.

When you have some ideas about what you want to do, find out:
- What the job involves.
- What (further) qualifications you need.

- What qualifications you will get whilst working.
- What training you will be given.
- What the prospects are for promotion or moving on.

? How do I find a job?

Careers offices

These are one of the best sources of local jobs for young people.

Local papers

If you can, get hold of the local papers from neighbouring areas as well.

Job centres

Many types of jobs are advertised here. If you can't see what you want, ask.

The internet

Many organisations have very useful websites.

Employment agencies

If you have work experience or a skill, such as typing, agencies may take you onto their books.

Personal contacts

Ask friends and relatives to keep their eyes open and tell you about any suitable vacancies that come up.

Many schools will have access to the Internet for job searching or you can do it at home or at Internet cafes.

When jobs are not easy to find it is especially important you take a lot of care with your applications.

? How do I apply for a job?

Many applications are available to download but if they are not, follow the instructions in the advert. It may require you to write in, telephone or email.

If the advertisement tells you to 'Write for an application form' then it means do not telephone. Your letter may however be typed or printed from a computer. If it says 'Apply in your own hand writing' then it must not be typed.

You may see a job advertised that you think you would like and could do but do not have the qualifications then write and tell them about yourself explaining exactly what you have to offer. They may be able to offer you something else or keep you in mind when they have a suitable vacancy.

It may be that the qualifications asked for are only a guideline. It may be the employer is confused about the different qualifications. This happened recently when a job was advertised asking for 'A' level maths. When a teacher telephoned and explained details of 'A' level maths the company soon realised that the job did not call for that level of ability.

If you see a job that you want to apply for advertised in the job centre, the staff there will either arrange an interview for you or tell you how to apply if they think you are suitable for the job.

If you have to telephone:
- Be prepared to explain why you want the job and what skills you have to offer.
- If you are using a public telephone use a phonecard so that your money doesn't run out in the middle of your call or if you are using your mobile phone make sure you have enough credit available.
- Don't hang up if you hear an answering machine – leave your name and details of where you can be contacted.

If you have to write:
- You should say clearly what job you are applying for, where you saw it advertised and ask for an application form. There will usually be a reference number for the post which you must quote.
- Give three or four reasons why you should be considered for the job.

Keep a copy of your application form!

Preparing your CV

CV stands for curriculum vitae. The term is Latin. The dictionary definition says a CV is the course of one's life. Many companies and organisations ask for a CV when you apply for a job or you could send it to a company to see whether you are suitable for any job they may have. A CV is a way of telling an employer about yourself in a simple and easy to read way. The important thing about a CV is that it must be:
- Accurate – without even the smallest 'white lie'.
- Easy to read – make it look good or different. It may be the reason why your CV receives attention over many others that have been sent.
- Up-to-date.
- With no spelling or typing mistakes – use spell check or get someone else to check it for you before you send it out.

You will need to ask one or two people to act as referees on your CVs – you could ask a teacher, a social worker, your doctor, or someone for whom you have worked before – people who know you reasonably well, and who you think will speak positively and honestly about you. They may be asked to comment on your character, and your suitability for the job you are applying for. Every time you give the names of the referees when applying for a job, you should tell the people concerned, giving brief details of the job you have applied for.

Always keep a copy so you can:
- Read it before an interview.
- Up-date it when necessary.
- Use it as a help when filling in a job application form.

There are many different ideas about the best way to write a CV. The following is just one example:

CURRICULUM VITAE

NAME	**AGE**	**DATE OF BIRTH**
Samantha Brooks	15	23rd June 1998

ADDRESS
26 St. John's Avenue
Fareham
Hampshire
PO25 1XX

TELEPHONE NUMBER
0123 0000

EDUCATION AND TRAINING
2007-2012: Ballharbour School

I will be taking the following exams in June:

Subject:	**Type of Examination:**
English	GCSE
Mathematics	GCSE
Geography	GCSE
Biology	GCSE
Music	GCSE

I have also gained my bronze life-saving award.

EMPLOYMENT AND WORK EXPERIENCE
I have worked in Newswell newsagents on Saturdays since November 2011.

INTERESTS
I enjoy badminton and swimming and I also help run the school aerobics club.
I am a member of the school choir and I play the piano to grade 3 standard.

REFEREES

Mrs. P. Green
Head of School
Ballharbour School
Smarts Lane
Fareham PO23 2YZ
Tel. 01234 567890

Mr. S. Singh
(Manager of Newswell)
42 Station Road
Portsmouth
PO1 1ZZ
Tel. 01987 65321

What is a person specification?

When some companies or organisations have a vacancy for a job they draw up and send out a person specification highlighting the qualities they are looking for in their employee. If this happens, you may need help with this application to show that you have the particular qualities – you may not think you have or be confident enough to say so – ask your carer to help.

The important thing to remember about a person specification is that if it indicates that a certain quality is essential, you must ensure you show evidence in your application of this. Your application will not be shortlisted for the interview otherwise.

Job interviews

Before going to an interview you should:
- Find out what you can about the job and the company.
- Talk over with your social worker, your carer, keyworker or personal adviser, mentor or teacher why you want the job and what you can offer.
- Decide in advance what you are going to wear and get it ready. If you aren't sure what to wear, ask your carer. Wear something that is comfortable but smart.
- Make sure you know exactly where the interview will be and how long it will take you to get there, so that you arrive in good time.
- Look at the copy you have of your application form to remind yourself of what you have said.
- When you arrive say you have come for an interview and ask at the reception desk where you should go. You will be shown where to wait.

At the interview

Below is a list of hints to give a young person who is going to an interview:
- Be friendly to everyone that you meet from the company but not too friendly.
- When you go in, look at the interviewer and shake their hand if they offer their hand to you. A handshake that is too bold may be considered a bit much, but a wet wishy one is worse! Only sit down when asked.
- Don't chew gum.
- Sit in a straight and upright (but relaxed) position and don't fidget.
- Think before you reply and then answer the question fully, not just 'yes' and 'no'.
- Take a pen and paper and write down some questions. It may help you to answer more fully and this can make a good impression.
- Be alert and interested. Sound positive and enthusiastic.
- At the end of the interview, thank the interviewer and say goodbye.

Typical interview questions:
- Why do you want to work for us?
- What have you got to offer?
- What were your favourite subjects at school?
- What are your long-term aims?

Practise some of these questions in advance until you are confident of your response especially as they could very easily be the first questions asked and it will help if you begin your interview well.

At the end of the interview you may be asked if you have any questions, so prepare some in advance. If you can't think of anything, just say 'I think you covered everything I need to know'. Before you leave try to find out when you will hear the result.

If there are two people interviewing you at the same time, speak to whoever asks you the question.

Getting an offer

After the interview you might get a job offer either by phone, email or in writing. If you are offered a job and you want to take it, contact them immediately saying thank you for the offer and how pleased you are to accept it. However, get someone to read the contract and any other documents included before you sign them.

If you decide not to accept the offer, get back and say so as soon as possible.

You may get asked to come back for another interview. This may be with the same interviewer or with somebody you have not met before.

Getting a rejection

Ask the company why you were not successful. Think about the reasons why you were not chosen and learn from the experience so that you are well prepared for the next interview you get. We all get rejection throughout our lives – do not be disheartened but try and work out what you can learn from the experience.

Hearing nothing at all

If you have heard nothing within two weeks, telephone or email and ask whether a decision has been made.

Review sheet

It's a good idea to keep a record of the job applications you have made.

You could include:
- name of company
- job title
- date of application
- date reply received
- action
- results
- comments

How to keep your job!

Once a young person has a job, the important thing is to help them keep it.

❓ *When I start work, what do I need to know?*

Many young people will have lived unsettled lives and the discipline and the stress of going to work will not come easy. Do you remember your first day at work? Talk it through with them and also remind them of such essentials as:

- Good time-keeping – not just at the start of the day but after breaks
- Attendance – good attendance is a must, but if you *really are* too ill to go to work, either you should phone in or you must get someone else to explain the situation and say when you may be expected back.
- Asking if they don't understand – no-one minds repeating something but they will mind incorrect work.
- Everyone makes mistakes – own up promptly and provided mistakes don't happen too often no one will mind too much, particularly for new staff.
- You will be the junior and may not be spoken to as you should – this is not right but may happen. 'Bite your tongue' and do not react except in extreme circumstances – think first, count to 10.

Many jobs, especially in the early days may be boring – don't give up, as:

- If you stick at it you may well be given a better job when one is available.
- You will actually feel quite pleased with yourself, and it should give you added confidence and self-respect.
- It's easier to get another job when you're in a job than if you're unemployed.
- It will be a useful talking point at another interview.
- You will probably get a reference from your first employer.

A young person may need to try several jobs before settling into the right one for them. They will need all the help and encouragement you can give them.

❓ *What if I think I'm being discriminated against?*

At work young people may find they are victims of discrimination. They may need your help to handle this and to know their rights.

Discrimination in any form is not acceptable. There are also a variety of laws which make discrimination illegal and your local Citizen's Advice Bureau (CAB) will be able to give more information and advise you about making a claim if this is appropriate. You could speak to the person at work responsible for staff, often called the human resources manager, or a union representative if there is one.

Keeping up appearances

In most jobs, appearance and personal hygiene are important and many young people find looking clean, tidy and smart all the time difficult. Help them to understand that they are now representing their company and must create the right image. Help them in practical ways by making sure that they have room to hang their clothes properly and to wash and iron them. Advise them on the best material to choose for any new clothes they buy or on their make-up, jewellery or hairstyle.

If they are in a job where their work clothes get very dirty they may think there is no point in changing them regularly. If clothes are not changed and the young person does not wash properly, they will smell – and this is unacceptable.

The young person's social worker may be involved in some of this work.

Apprenticeships

Apprenticeships are an excellent way of gaining qualifications and workplace experience. As an employee, you can earn as you learn and you gain practical skills from the workplace.

There may be different entry requirements for apprenticeships depending on your job choice.

Apprenticeships are open to all age groups above 16 years old whether you are just leaving school, have been working for years or are seeking to start a new career.

Competition for places can be fierce, so you will need to show that you are committed, and aware of your responsibilities to both yourself and the company.

You also need to be happy to work as both part of a team and individually, and be able to use your own initiative.

Apprenticeships are increasingly recognised as the gold standard for work-based training.

There are three levels of apprenticeship available for those aged 16 and over:
1. Apprenticeships
2. Advanced apprenticeships
3. Higher apprenticeships

Apprenticeships
- Apprentices work towards work-based learning qualifications such as an NVQ Level 2, key skills and, in some cases, a relevant knowledge-based qualification such as a BTEC.
- These provide the skills you need for your chosen career and allow entry to an advanced apprenticeship.

Advanced apprenticeships
- Advanced apprentices work towards work-based learning qualifications such as NVQ Level 3, key skills and, in most cases, a relevant knowledge-based certificate such as a BTEC.
- To start this programme, you should ideally have five GCSEs (grade C or above) or have completed an apprenticeship.

Higher apprenticeships
- Higher apprenticeships work towards work-based learning qualifications such as NVQ Level 4 and, in some cases, a knowledge-based qualification such as a foundation degree.

Going to college full time is an important choice for many young people. As an apprentice it may be that you will be expected to attend college part time.

Feeling isolated and lonely: support networks

The following could provide useful support, information and resources for anyone no longer in care:

- The Who cares? Trust
- care leavers groups
- other people who have been looked after
- family and relatives
- Samaritans where young people can talk to trained counsellors in private
- their carers
- other people who have been helpful in the past
- local after-care group
- ex-teachers
- local drop-in centres
- youth leader
- community groups
- church, temple or mosque
- old school friend

? *What practical things would help?*

There are many practical ways in which you as a carer can make the transition to independent living seem less daunting. Encourage young people to:

- Use social networking sites responsibly.
- Keep an address book or e-mail contacts list with names, e-mail addresses, home addresses and telephone numbers of families, friends and any others in the above list.
- Swap addresses and e-mails with friends.
- Let everyone know their new address or e-mail if they move on or change details.
- Give an address of someone who will know where they are: as someone may want to get in contact with them.

Keeping your belongings safe

On average £500 in electronic gear, more if they have guitars etc., are owned by a young person when they leave home or go to university.

Allianz Insurance

Young people need guidance to make sure they are not creating a 'muggers paradise'. They need to know how to keep their property, and of course, their accommodation as safe as possible. They will also need insurance to cover any loss.

Independence checklist

The aim of the checklist on the following pages is to find out what a young person knows and how ready they are for independence. Some young people may need your help to read it or fill it in. Others may flatly refuse. This may reflect their anxiety about moving on so they may need additional help and support. Other young people may say it is intrusive but if you explain the reasons for both of them and you needing to know this information hopefully they will accept it. You can then both work on the areas of concern together.

The questions are not so much 'can they do this?' as 'do they do this?'.

The questionnaire may be filled in one go, or in stages. They can go back and add or change things whenever they wish. It is not a test.

It can be photocopied and used again by the same young person in a year or so's time.

The areas covered are:
- Helping young people to build relationships with others.
- Helping young people to develop self-esteem.
- Practical and financial skills and knowledge.
- Their future.

The checklist also asks what they think about things: it is important for young people not just to have knowledge but to think about getting as much information and help as they can.
- Talk over the answers with them.
- Help them make a plan, with a time limit, of what help they would like.

✎ Independence checklist

Name ....

Age/Date of birth ....

Foster carer or keyworker ....

Date completed 1st time ....

Dates changes made ....

A. Education or employment

1. Which of the following are you doing? Circle the answer and state which school, college or workplace:

    •   local school/college – full or part-time

    •   further education – full or part-time

    •   work experience, how much? where?

    •   youth training, where?

    •   employed – full or part-time

    •   unemployed or registered with careers office

2. Would you say that you attended the above - regularly/more than half/less than half?

3. Why do you think your attendance is the way you say it is?

→

B. Social contact

1. Do you attend, belong to or take part in one or more of the following?

    • church/temple/mosque/synagogue – regularly/sometimes

    • local youth club – regularly/sometimes

    • sports club – regularly/sometimes

    • hobby or activity – regularly/sometimes

    • outdoor activity trips

    • Duke of Edinburgh Award – what level and what activities?

    • other

2. Is there any other outside event or place that you go to where you meet other people? (e.g. a disco, the town centre) How often?

3. Do you know of any places where you can get a discount on leisure schemes in your area? (If not, would you like help to find out?)

4. Do you have friends of your own age locally? Do they visit you, or you them?

    Have they stayed overnight at your house, or have you stayed at their place?

5. Do you have any older friends? Who?

C. Family

1. Which members of your family are you in touch with? For example: parents, brothers and sisters, step-parents, foster family. What type of contact – telephone? visits? How often?

2. Do you know about your family history?

3. Would you like to know more? If so what else would you like to know?

4. Do you know where to get more information?

5. Is there anyone you would like to contact or trace?

D. Achievements

1. What school or college qualifications have you got or are expecting to get?

2. What sports or hobby awards or certificates have you?

3. Have you done any other courses or training? (e.g. first aid)

4. What personal ambition or resolution have you achieved in the last year?

5. Have you attended any job interviews (including work experience)? Have you been offered a position?

ative?

E. Taking part in making decisions about leaving care

1. Do you have group meetings that you go to?

2. Do you attend your reviews? (date of last one)

3. Which area do you want to live in, when you leave? Locally, or near your family if they live in a different area?

4. Would you choose to live with family, friends, foster carers or supported lodgings, in independent living units, or on your own?

F. Practical skills

Reading, writing and maths

1. Do you read a newspaper or magazine? Which one? (If not, would you like to?)

2. Do you understand job adverts in the paper? (If not would you like help to?)

3. Can you write a letter? (e.g. applying for a job) (If not would you like help to?)

4. Have you got a CV (personal information sheet) for job applications? (If not would you like help to make one?)

5. Can you read and follow a recipe? Instructions on packets?

6. Can you add up a shopping price list?

7. Have you made a budget for a week's shopping?

8. Which of the following bills have you seen? Food, clothes, electric, gas, water rates, TV licence, council tax, telephone, and rent (as part of a written agreement). Do you understand all/any of them? If not, would you like some help?

→

Shopping

1. How do you buy your clothes? Circle
   (a) Adult buys them
   (b) They pay, you choose
   (c) You shop independently
   (d) Mail order

2. Do you go food shopping with adults?

   Do you choose some of the menus?

3. How often do you go and where?

4. Have you been food shopping on your own? Where? How often?

Preparing food and cooking

1. Are you able to use a cooker safely? Gas? Electric?

2. Do you help prepare or cook meals? How often?

3. Can you cook a hot meal for yourself? What? When?

4. Do you plan what you are going to eat so you get a balanced diet? Would you like some help?

5. Have you been shown how to use a fridge or freezer? (how long food keeps etc.)

6. Do you lay the table? When?

   Wash up? When?

→

Household

1. Can you change a light bulb or fuse?

2. Can you unblock a sink? Know what a stop-cock is?

3. Have you sewn on a button? Can you do other simple mending of clothes?

4. Can you read a meter? Can you check the electricity, water and gas bills?

5. Do you use the telephone? Payphone? Mobile phone? Can you check the bill to ensure it is correct?

6. Can you use a calculator? Have you got one?

7. Can you measure? length; weight; fluid?

8. Can you do simple first aid? What?

9. Can you mend a puncture on a bike?

G   **Managing money**

1. What is your weekly income? (pocket money, earnings?)

2. Do you save any? How?

3. Do you pay something towards your keep?

4. What do you spend the rest on?

5. Are you given any other cash by the adults (e.g. travel, leisure)?

6. Do you borrow? How you do pay back?

7. Do you spend money on anything you wish that you didn't? What? Would you like help to stop?

H Health and health education

1. Who is your doctor? dentist?

2. How do you arrange to see them?

3. If you move to another area, you will need to register with another doctor. Do you know how to do this?

4. Do you know where to find your National Health Card?

5. Have you been given enough information on the following? (Circle)

   - sex education/contraception
   - drugs – legal and illegal
   - rights
   - religion
   - social security
   - HIV/AIDS
   - the police
   - racism
   - housing

6. By whom, and when? Would you like any more information on any of these subjects?

7. Do you have books or leaflets on any of the above? Which? Where?

8. Do you have any local telephone numbers where you can make contact about any problems you may have?

9. Have you someone you can talk to about these topics?

→

I.   Privacy

1.   Have you keys for a) the front door? b) your room? c) other?

2.   Do you have your own bedroom?

3.   Do you have a safe and secure place to keep valuables? Where?

4.   Do you have somewhere that you consider to be private?

5.   Are you able to be in and be alone?

J.   General Information and Rights

1.   Are you a member of the library? Do you use it?

2.   Do you know where these other agencies are? What are their telephone numbers?

   - police station

   - dept. of social security

   - housing offices

   - careers office

   - employment service (job centre)

   - doctors' surgery

   - health clinic

   - Samaritans

   - citizens advice bureau

3.   Do you know how to complain if things are not right?

4.   Who is your social worker?

5.   Have you got their address and telephone number?

6. Do you know what to do if stopped by the police or arrested?

7. Do you know you can get free legal advice? Would you like help?

8. Do you know how to get in touch with an appropriate adult? Would you like help?

9. Do you know where to find your birth certificate? and National Insurance Number?

10. Do you know at what age the law allows you to:
    - smoke
    - drink alcohol
    - get married
    - have sex
    - vote
    - appear in adult court

11. Have you been given careers advice – how to apply for a job or use the job centre?

12. When you are 16 you can put your name on the electoral register. You will then be able to vote when you are 18. Do you know how to get on the register? Do you need help?

K. Feeling Isolated

1. Do you know where to go for help if you really feel bad about something or someone or just feel lonely?

2. Have you got an address book with names and telephone numbers in?

3. Have you some ideas on how to overcome loneliness? What are they?

4. If there is a crisis in your life, such as breaking up with your long standing boy or girlfriend, what would you do?

5. Do you know how to go about making new friends?

→

L. Nationality and ethnicity

1. Do you know what your nationality is?

2. If you are not British, do you know if anything needs to be done to sort out your immigration, citizenship and nationality status?

3. Do you have all the documents needed for future dealings over passport, immigration etc.?

4. Do you know who can help?

5. Have you got an up-to-date passport?

6. Do you know who will be able to sign the form to support your application for a passport?

7. Do you know which ethnic group you come from?

8. If you come from a minority ethnic group do you need help to meet more people from the same ethnic background?

Is there anything else that has not been asked that you think is important?

Your carer and social worker may be able to help you with some of this information. You could use the Internet to find out some other information.

(Adapted from *Leaving Care from Therapeutic Communities*, unpublished thesis by James Cathcart, University of Southampton, 1992)

Introduction

Most young people will never attend court in their life and will never have a court order that refers to them. Unfortunately this is not true for many young people who are looked after. Going to court or having a court order placed on them can be very distressing. One way of helping a young person to better understand the situation is to give them as much information as possible. This section sets out what many of the legal terms mean, but it does not cover criminal law.

Carers see the young person on a day-to-day basis and have valuable information about them. For the sake of the young person it is vital that foster carers are well prepared and should they be called to attend court hearings: the following tips could be useful:

- **Know the legal status:** This means understanding the range of orders that the court can make, or have made, concerning the young person. The order will cover such things as contact with parents and many more (see the rest of this section for details).

- **Understand the role of the children's guardian (safeguarder or curator ad litem)** page 177.

- **Keep records and have them with you in court:** Keeping records of such things as placement agreements, reviews, correspondence: even your own hand written observations can be extremely valuable in proving a point or establishing facts in court. A foster carer who is 'organised' will always be viewed in a better light than one who is not.

- **Attend reviews and conferences about the young person:** You have a right to attend these meetings and at them you will learn what applications and recommendations are to be made to the court, as well as gaining other useful information about the young person.

- **Understand the importance of documentary evidence:** All cases involving young people rely heavily on documentary evidence, hence the need for records to be kept. You may be required to write to the court and if so it is wise to seek the help of a legal advisor. Make sure however that you write in your own words, do not let anyone put in jargon or technical language.

- **Know who will be in court:** In the Family Proceedings Court there will be three magistrates. There will be a clerk to guide proceedings and take notes. In County and High Courts there will be a person to record what is said but the judge runs the court. There will be an usher to call you in and you will be invited to swear an oath on a holy book or to 'affirm' if you do not wish to swear on a holy book.

Being in care, being accommodated or being on remand

There are three main ways a young person becomes looked after:

1. **Being in care:** This means that a court order has been issued (see following pages for details of the different types of orders). Parental responsibility will be shared between the

local authority and the parents. All decisions made about a young person should be made in consultation with the young person and the parents if possible.

2. **Being accommodated:** Usually a young person under 16 may only be accommodated with the consent of the parents or those with parental responsibility. It is entirely voluntary and there is no court order. There may be some circumstances where a young person under the age of 16 can seek to be accommodated.

3. **Being on remand:** A young person can be remanded to local authority accommodation from the age of 10, which is the age of criminal responsibility.

Children's services provide somewhere for a young person to live if:

- There is no one who has parental responsibility for the young person.
- The young person has been lost or abandoned or has been thrown out of home.
- The person caring for the young person cannot provide accommodation or care either temporarily or permanently.
- The young person might suffer ill-treatment from another person.

The Children Act 1989, The Children (Scotland) Act 1995 and The Children (Northern Ireland) Order 1995

It may be necessary for the young person to go to court if, for example, their parents and social services can't agree on the best plan for their safety and well-being in the future. Court orders are only made when the best interests of the young person can be achieved by that order, and when it is better than making no order. In Scotland, a Children's Hearing may convene but at present young people may not attend. Carers may need to:

- Explain to the young person the reasons for attendance at court.
- Explain the decisions the court could make.
- Prepare the young person for going to court.

If there is a court order it will automatically end when a young person is 18 unless it is discharged by the court earlier, the young person is adopted or the young person marries.

There should be a Children's Guardian (curator ad litem or safeguarder in Scotland) appointed to talk about the young person's wishes and feelings. In addition a solicitor will be appointed to represent the young person. If the young person is of sufficient understanding they may attend the court with the solicitor. Occasionally the Children's Guardian will appoint their own solicitor if there is a differing of opinions. Carers should ensure that the young person's view is heard. An interpreter may be necessary. Young people are looked after by the local authority if they are either accommodated or a court has made an order committing them to the care of the local authority.

The court must:

- Consider what is best for the young person including contact with families.
- Make sure that whatever is to happen, happens as soon as possible.
- See that nothing changes unless it is better for the young person.

The court must also consider:

- What the young person wants and any needs the young person may have.

- What the effect will be on the young person of any changes.
- The age, sex, background, race, culture, language or anything else that might be important to the young person such as their brothers and sisters.
- Any problems there may have been in the past or are likely to be in future.
- The ability of the parents, guardians or carers to meet those needs.

On the following pages there is a brief explanation of the various orders that might be imposed.

Court orders: a summary of what they mean

Emergency Protection Order (EPO)

This is made if the court has reason to believe that:
- Young people will come to immediate significant harm if they continue to live where they are or if they are removed from where they are staying.
- They are suffering significant harm and their parents or carers will not allow doctors or social workers to see them and the harm is likely to continue if they are not removed.

The order cannot be stopped or challenged within the first 72 hours. After that it may be challenged in court providing the parent or carer was not present at the initial hearing. It can last up to eight days and then be extended for a further seven days. The young person may be asked to have a medical examination, either physical or psychiatric, but may refuse provided they fully understand what is going on. This refusal can be overridden under certain circumstances.

Exclusion Order (Scotland only)

This is made to allow the alleged abuser to be removed from the home rather than the young person.

Interim Care Order (ICO)

An Interim Care Order will often follow an Emergency Protection Order. This gives the court time to collect more information and is normally made for not more than eight weeks. Sometimes further ICOs can be made which will last up to four weeks each. There should be as few ICOs as possible to avoid delay in making a final decision. The young person may be asked to have a medical examination, either physical or psychiatric, but can refuse provided they fully understand. Usually parents will have contact with their child under ICOs.

Care Order

This is made by the court and states the local authority must look after the young person and provide accommodation. A care order gives children's services parental responsibility jointly with the parents. Young people should be encouraged to see their families and friends unless the court states otherwise. A care order is made if the court thinks the young person might be:
- Suffering significant harm or likely to suffer significant harm, this includes witnessing or being affected by domestic violence.
- The care being given is not what a parent should give or the young person is beyond the parents' control.

It lasts until one of the following happens:
- The young person reaches the age of 18.
- The young person is adopted.
- The young person marries.
- The young person, their parents, children's services or the person with parental responsibility asks the court to discharge the order and the court agrees. The court may then make a Supervision Order, Residence Order or a Special Guardianship Order.

Residence Order

This is a court order stating with whom the young person must live. It lasts usually until the young person is 16 but occasionally until the young person is 18 years old. Foster carers can apply for a Residence Order for a young person they have cared for but will need the support of the local authority and will need to have cared for the young person for three years. A Residence Order means:
- The young person must live with whoever is specified in the order and that person will be given parental responsibility if they haven't got it already. This will be shared with anybody else who has parental responsibility.
- The young person cannot leave the country for more than a month (nor can the young person change their surname) without the written permission of whoever has parental responsibility or the court.
- Any interested party can apply to have it stopped at any time.

Special Guardianship Order (SGO)

This order usually lasts until the young person is 16 or 18 under special circumstances and gives the carer shared parental responsibility. In agreement with the local authority foster carers can apply for a SGO after the young person has been in placement for a year and an SGO should be accompanied by a support package for the young person drawn up and supported by the local authority.

Adoption

There are over half a million adopted people living in Britain today. Young people aged 12-18 are not adopted very often at present. Adoption is usually for the younger child, but sometimes, young people in the 12-18 age group may want to know about adoption.

? What is an Adoption Order?

This court order gives adopters full legal rights to a child. The child will have the same rights and status as a birth child and this is granted when the court is satisfied that an adoption can go ahead.

? What is a Placement Order?

This means that the young person has been released from their birth parents' responsibility in preparation for being adopted but must be looked after by children's services until the adoption is finalised. It also means that they are protected and no one can do anything until the court decides whether or not an adoption can go ahead.

? *What is an adoption panel?*

This is a group of people, including someone from children's services, teachers, health visitors, someone from the adoption agency, who meet to make sure:

* The adoption is in the young person's best interests.
* The family is suitable to adopt.
* The young person is suitable for that family.

Children's Guardian (previously Guardian ad Litem (GAL), Curator ad Litem (CAL) or Safeguarder)

In Scotland when an application for adoption is made a curator ad litem may be appointed. Adoption cases may be heard in the Court of Session or more usually in the local sheriff court. At other times where a young person's case comes before a children's hearing, a safeguarder may be appointed. Much of the work of these two groups are similar to the role of the children's guardian.

? *What is Children's Guardian (Curator ad Litem or Safeguarder)?*

A children's guardian is a person who looks after a young person's interests if the matter is brought before the court. A children's guardian is appointed by the court, and does not work for children's services.

? *What do these people do?*

* Listen to what a young person wants now and for the future.
* Talk to the young person, the parents, grandparents and anyone else who is important to the young person.
* Talk to teachers, social workers, health visitors and anyone else who can give advice or help.
* Read reports about the young person and their family and provide a report to the court promoting the young person's interests.
* Work out what is best for the young person.

The guardian will choose a suitable solicitor who will be able to explain to the court what is best for the young person.

Guardians

They should not be confused with children's guardians.

? *What is a guardian then?*

A guardian is a person who is given full parental responsibility for a young person because the parents have died or are unable to care for the young person. The guardian will have the same responsibilities that their parents would have had.

? *Who can appoint a guardian?*

* Anyone with parental responsibility.
* Any other guardian.
* A court.

? *When does guardianship stop?*
- When the young person is 18.
- When the court orders it to stop.
- When either the young person or someone with parental responsibility applies to the court to have it stopped and the court agrees it is in the interest of the young person.

Parental responsibility

A young person's parents will always have parental responsibility for their young person unless the young person is adopted. The parental responsibility of the parents will be shared with the local authority if the local authority is granted an order from the court. This would usually be an Interim Care Order or a Care Order. In these circumstances the local authority will have the over-riding responsibility to make decisions for the young person but they must keep the young person's parents informed and consult with them.

Standards in foster care

The way England, Wales, Scotland and Northern Ireland have been devolved over the past years has resulted in variations in the way each country takes responsibility for social care. This has led to some marked differences, and one such is in the requirement to work with nationally proscribed standards. Please refer specifically to the website for each country's government department for more details. BAAF and the Fostering Network also work across the four countries, and are able to give more details.

Although there are differences in detail, the governments of England, Scotland, Wales and Northern Ireland all require that carers understand:
- The principles and values essential for fostering children and young people.
- Their role as a foster carer.
- Health and safety and health care.
- How to communicate effectively with children.
- The development of children and young people.
- How to keep children and young people safe from harm.
- The importance of self-development.

The aim of this book is to:
- Help all carers achieve the expectations placed on them and maintain good standards.
- Underline and encourage the use of relevant government standards.
- Give examples of good practice.